Mr. Mendoza's Paintbrush

Mr. Mendoza's Paintbrush

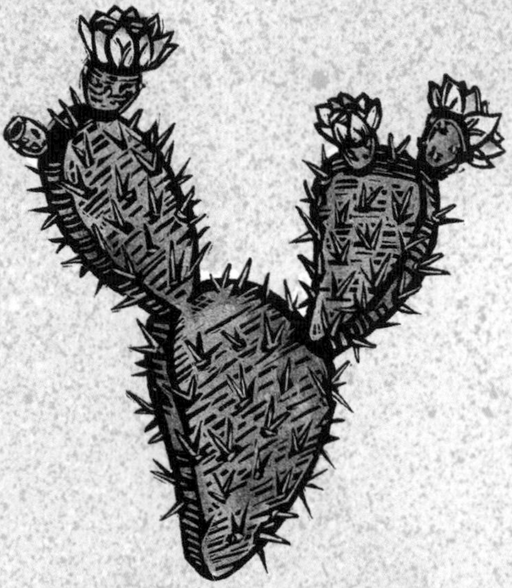

LUIS ALBERTO URREA

Artwork by

Christopher Cardinale

COLOR MASKING AND COMPOSITING

Anthony Cardinale

•

DESIGN

Anne M. Giangiulio

•

Cinco Puntos Press

For further information, write Cinco Puntos Press,
701 Texas Avenue, El Paso, TX 79901;
or call (915) 838-1625. Printed in Hong Kong.

FIRST EDITION
10 9 8 7 6 5 4 3 2 1

Library of Congress Cataloging-in-Publication Data

Urrea, Luis Alberto.
Mr. Mendoza's paintbrush / by Luis Alberto Urrea;
illustrated by Christopher Cardinale. — 1st ed.
p. cm.
ISBN 978-1-933693-23-1 (alk. paper)
1. Graphic novels. I. Cardinale, Christopher. II. Title.
PN6727.U77M7 2010
741.5'6973—dc22
2008011636

Mr. Mendoza's Paintbrush originally appeared in *Six Kinds of Sky*
by Luis Alberto Urrea (Cinco Puntos Press, 2002).

DEDICADO A:

EL RUBIO, EL EMBA, EL GUASAS, PINCHE FAUSTO,
LA NANCY, LA MELBA Y LA YRMA. AMEN.
—LUIS ALBERTO URREA

DEDICATED TO:

MY PARENTS P.J. AND BOB, MY BROTHER ANTHONY,
MY PARTNER SHARON AND MY SON MACEÓ,
WITH GRATITUDE AND LOVE.
—CHRISTOPHER CARDINALE

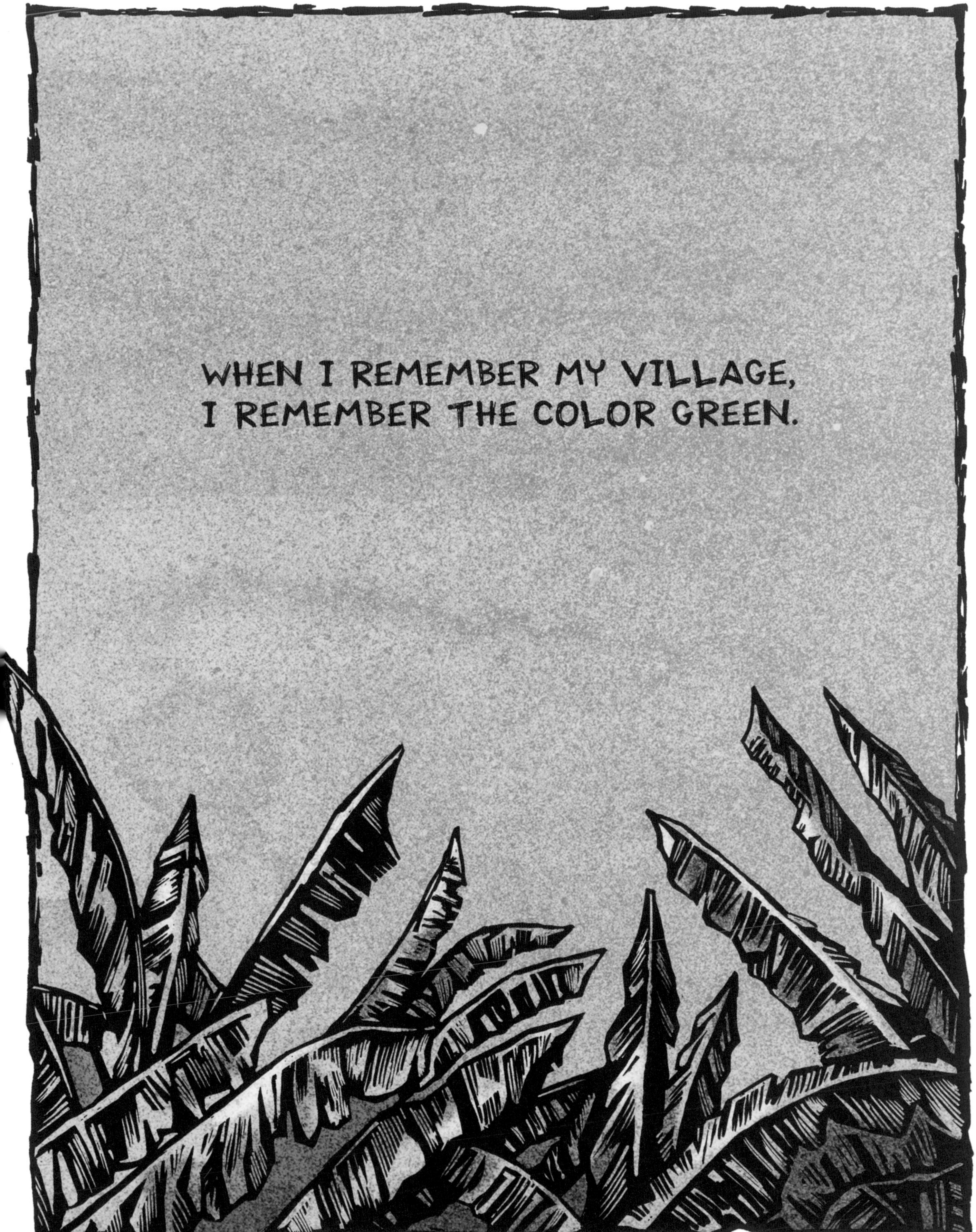
WHEN I REMEMBER MY VILLAGE,
I REMEMBER THE COLOR GREEN.

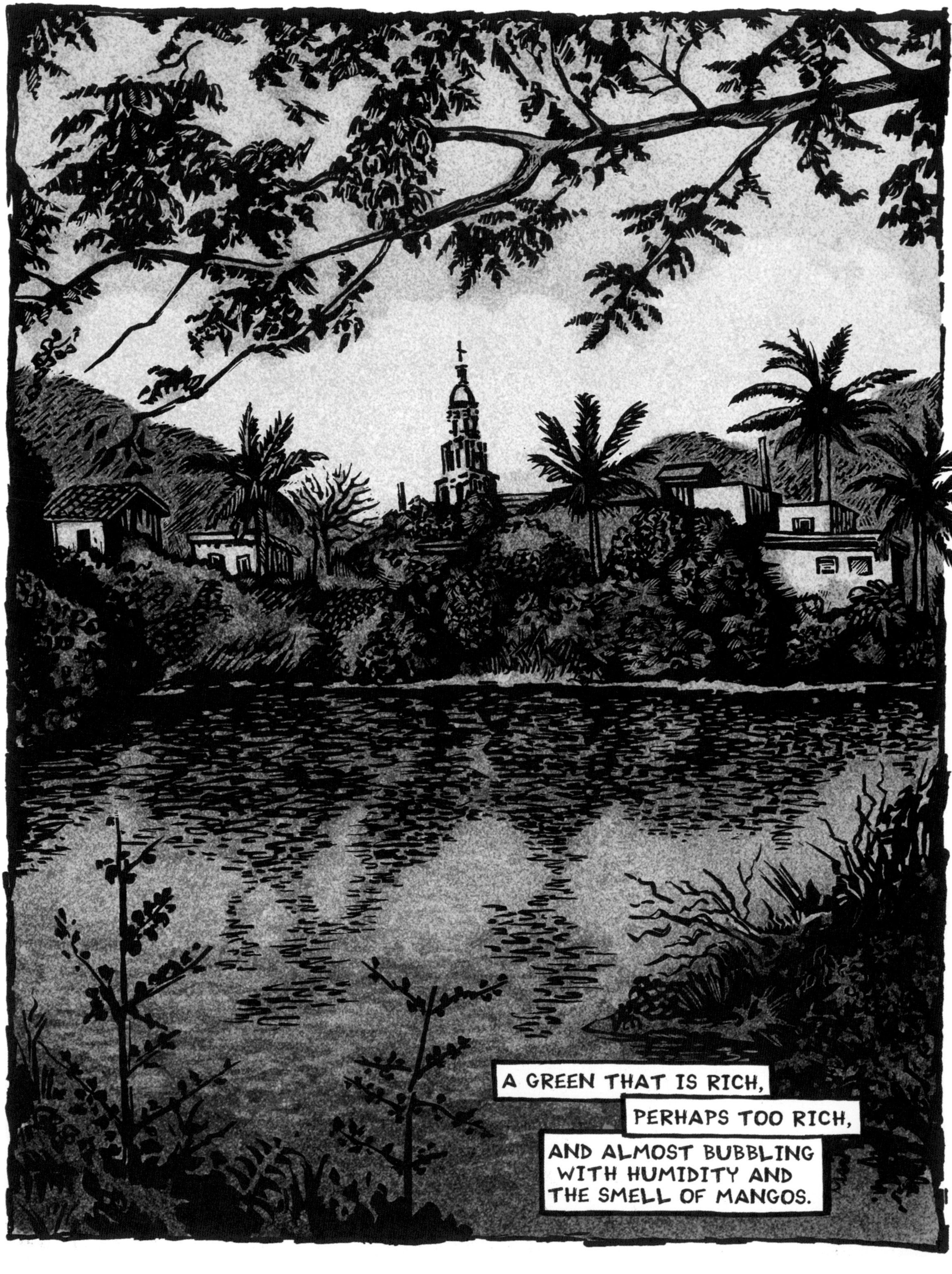
A GREEN THAT IS RICH,
PERHAPS TOO RICH,
AND ALMOST BUBBLING WITH HUMIDITY AND THE SMELL OF MANGOS.

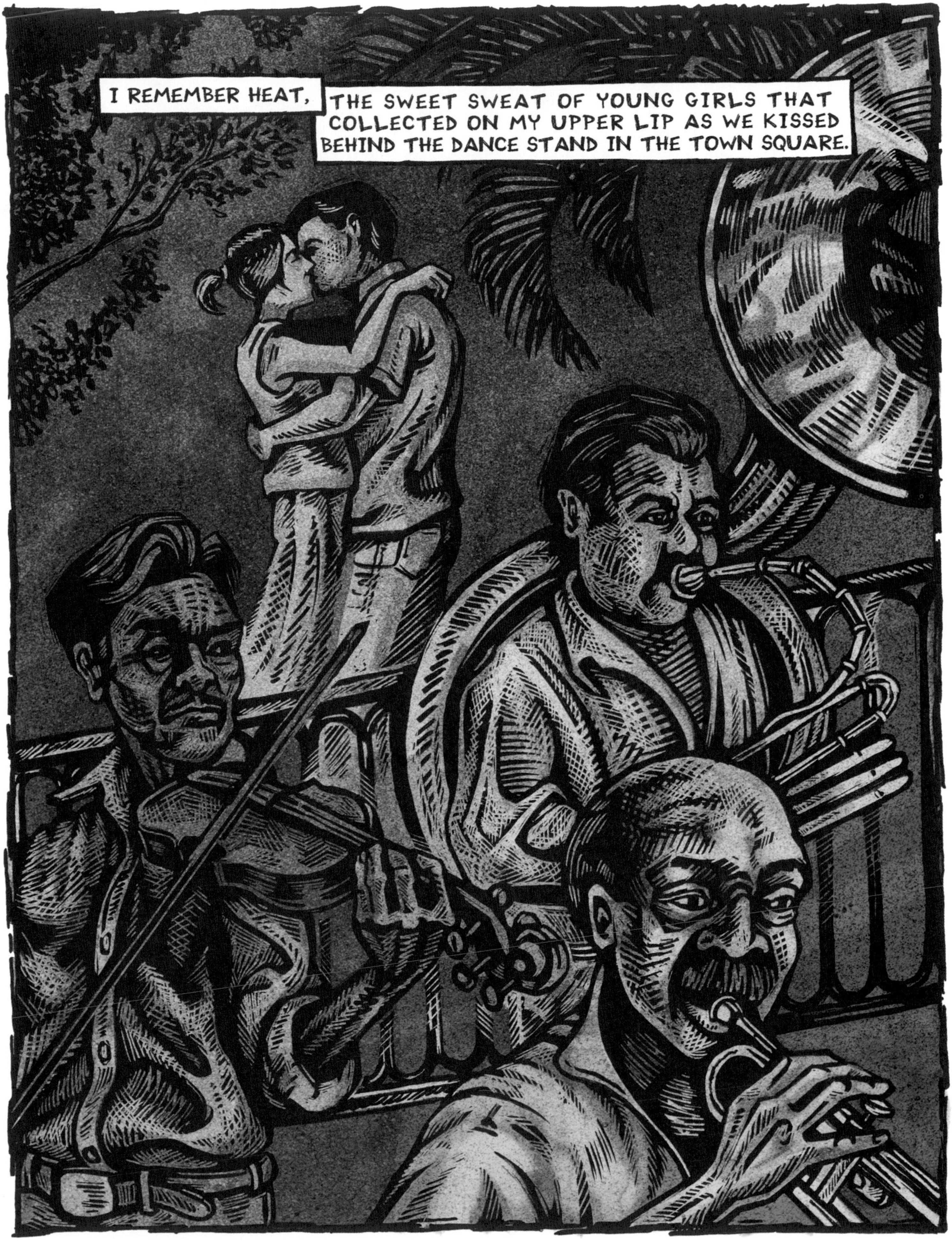
I REMEMBER HEAT,
THE SWEET SWEAT OF YOUNG GIRLS THAT COLLECTED ON MY UPPER LIP AS WE KISSED BEHIND THE DANCE STAND IN THE TOWN SQUARE.

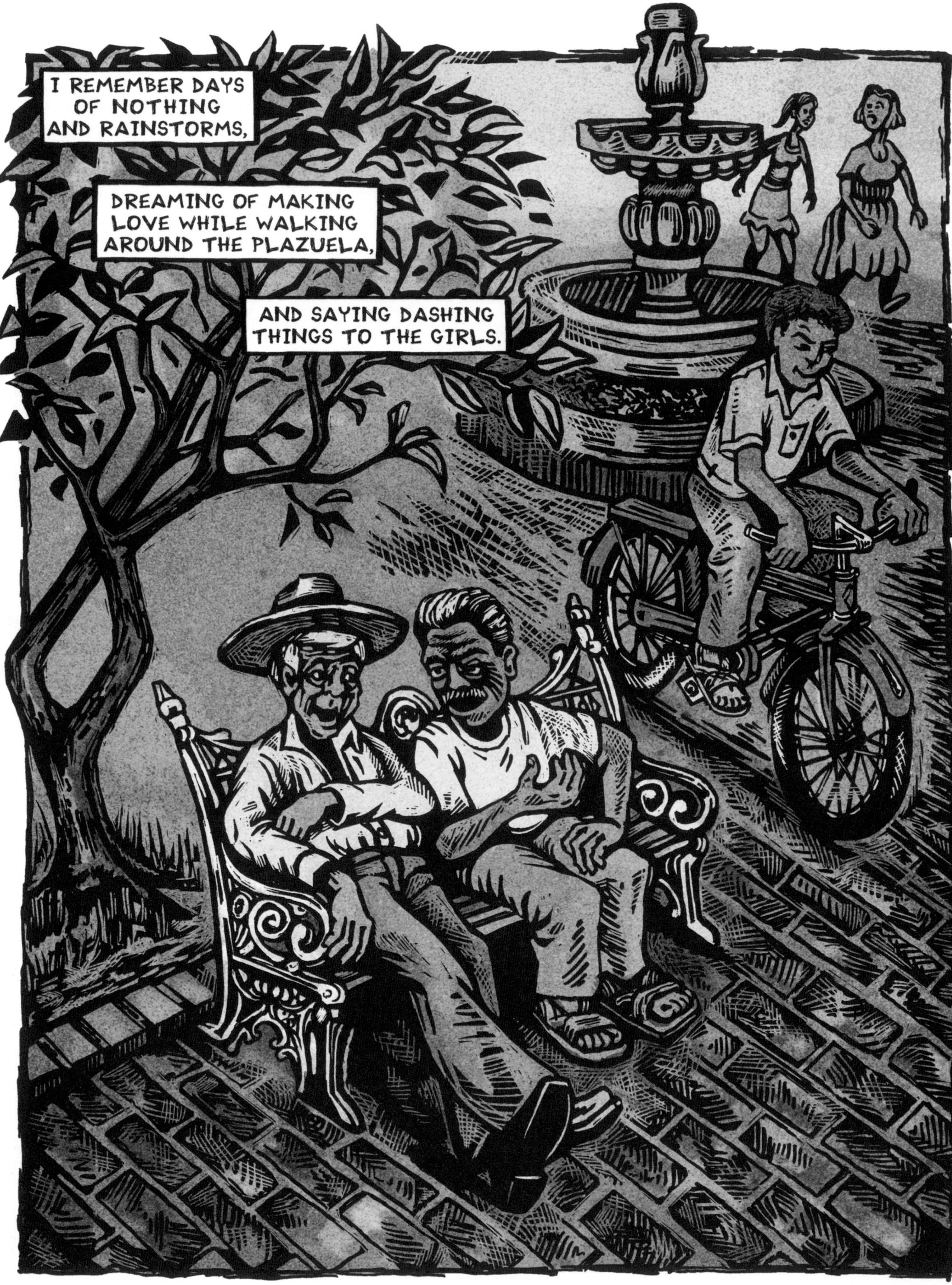
I REMEMBER DAYS OF NOTHING AND RAINSTORMS,
DREAMING OF MAKING LOVE WHILE WALKING AROUND THE PLAZUELA,
AND SAYING DASHING THINGS TO THE GIRLS.

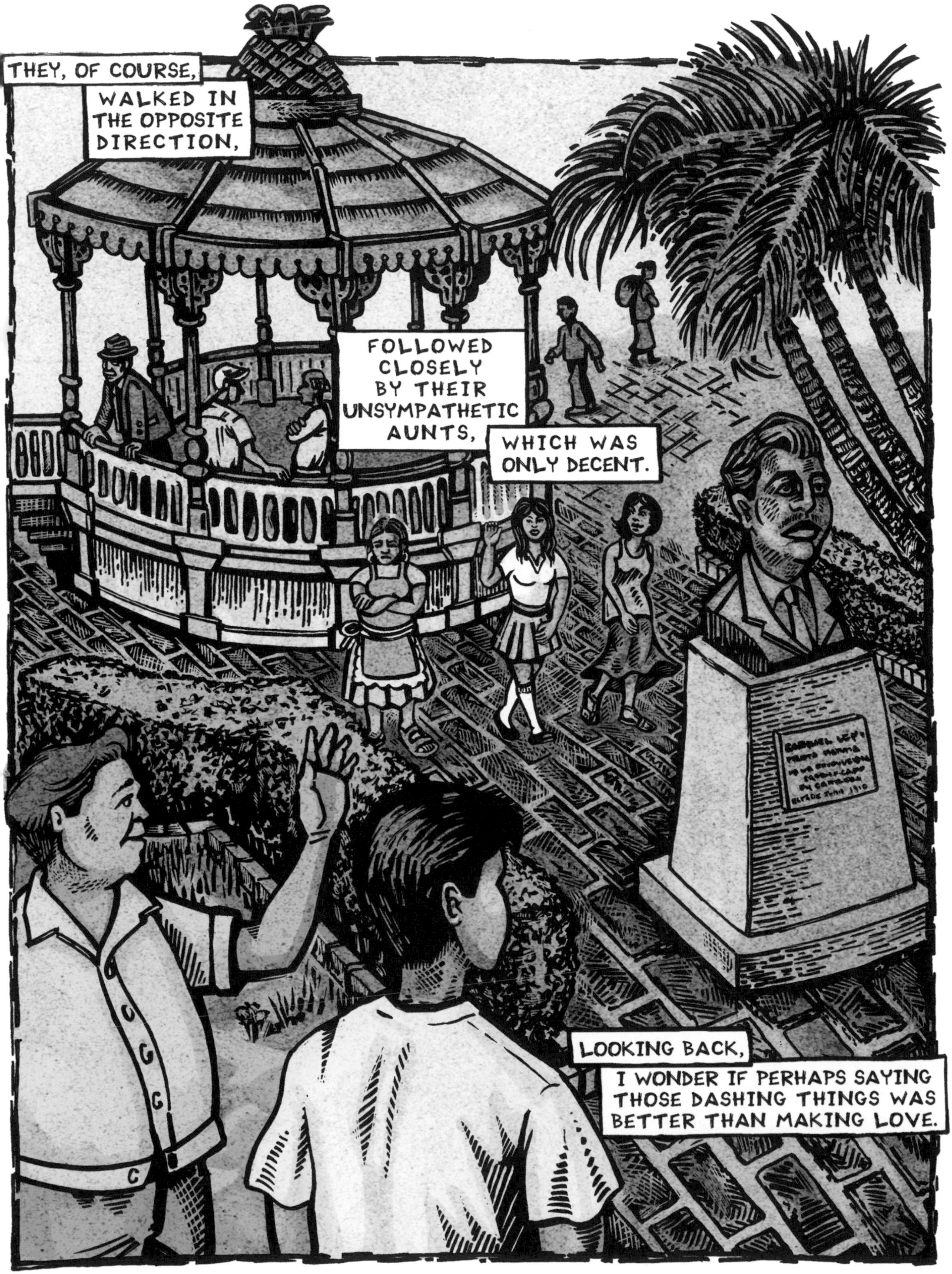
THEY, OF COURSE,
WALKED IN THE OPPOSITE DIRECTION,
FOLLOWED CLOSELY BY THEIR UNSYMPATHETIC AUNTS,
WHICH WAS ONLY DECENT.
LOOKING BACK,
I WONDER IF PERHAPS SAYING THOSE DASHING THINGS WAS BETTER THAN MAKING LOVE.

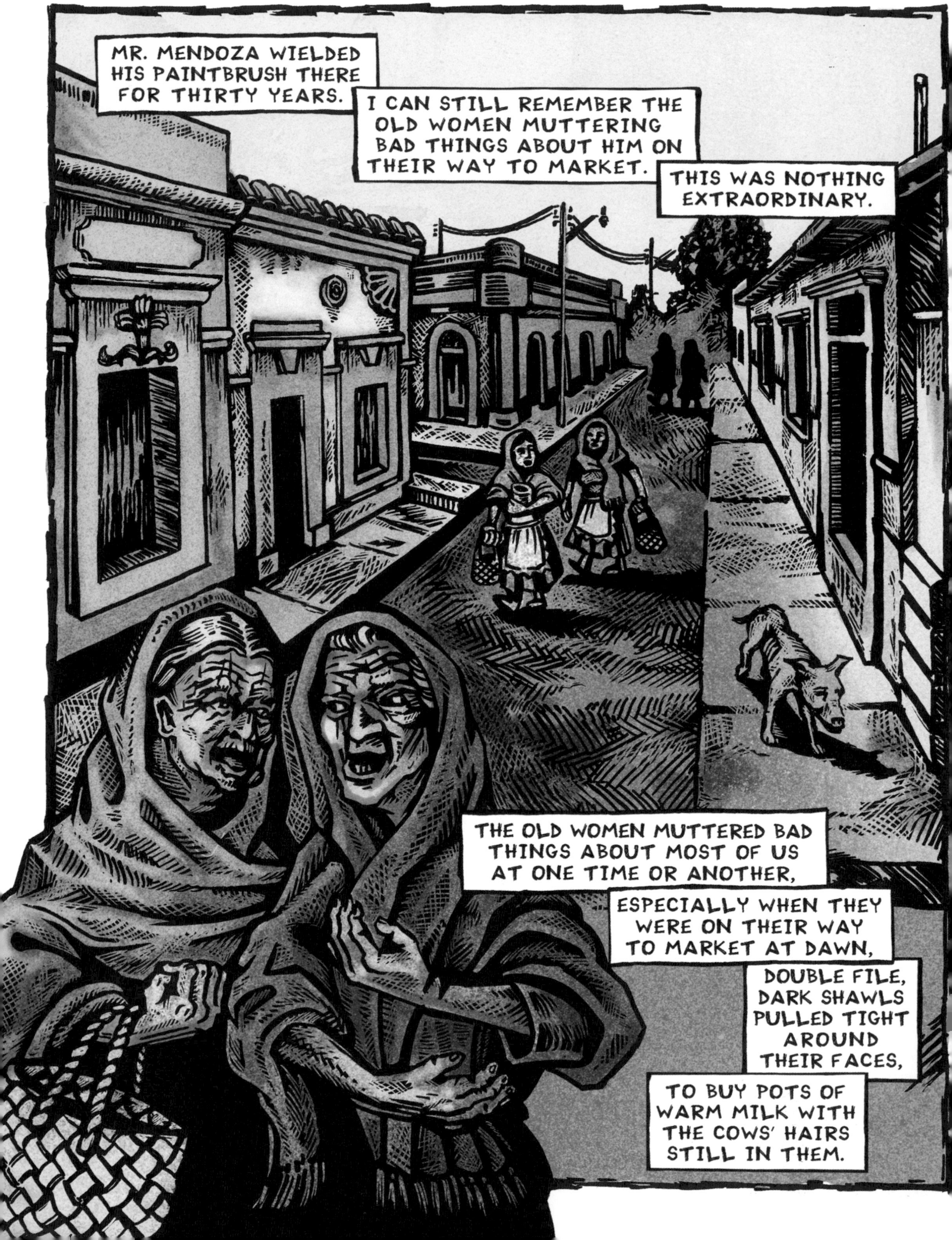
MR. MENDOZA WIELDED HIS PAINTBRUSH THERE FOR THIRTY YEARS.
I CAN STILL REMEMBER THE OLD WOMEN MUTTERING BAD THINGS ABOUT HIM ON THEIR WAY TO MARKET.
THIS WAS NOTHING EXTRAORDINARY.
THE OLD WOMEN MUTTERED BAD THINGS ABOUT MOST OF US AT ONE TIME OR ANOTHER,
ESPECIALLY WHEN THEY WERE ON THEIR WAY TO MARKET AT DAWN,
DOUBLE FILE, DARK SHAWLS PULLED TIGHT AROUND THEIR FACES,
TO BUY POTS OF WARM MILK WITH THE COWS' HAIRS STILL IN THEM.

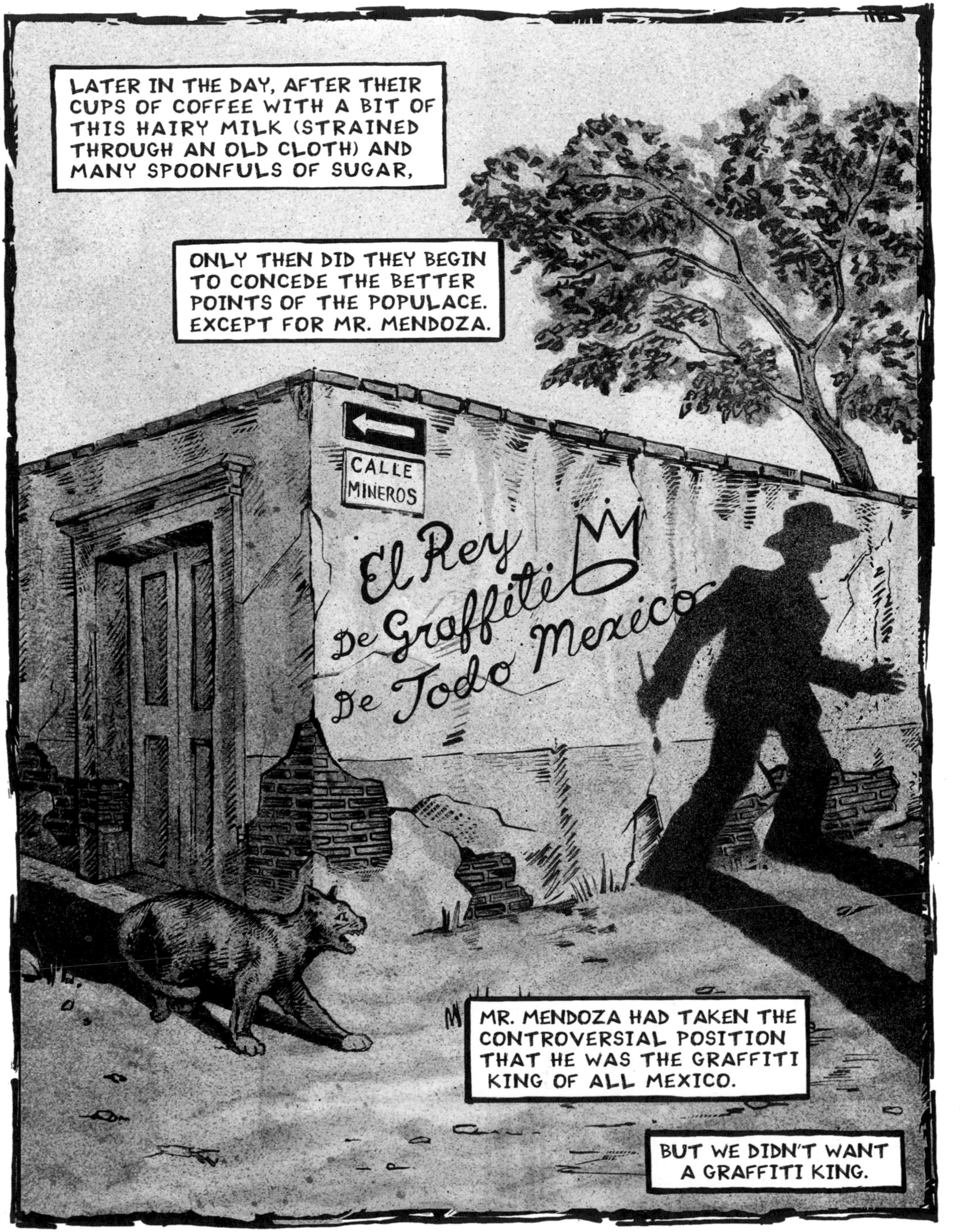
LATER IN THE DAY, AFTER THEIR CUPS OF COFFEE WITH A BIT OF THIS HAIRY MILK (STRAINED THROUGH AN OLD CLOTH) AND MANY SPOONFULS OF SUGAR,
ONLY THEN DID THEY BEGIN TO CONCEDE THE BETTER POINTS OF THE POPULACE. EXCEPT FOR MR. MENDOZA.
CALLE MINEROS
El Rey De Graffiti De Todo Mexico
MR. MENDOZA HAD TAKEN THE CONTROVERSIAL POSITION THAT HE WAS THE GRAFFITI KING OF ALL MEXICO.
BUT WE DIDN'T WANT A GRAFFITI KING.

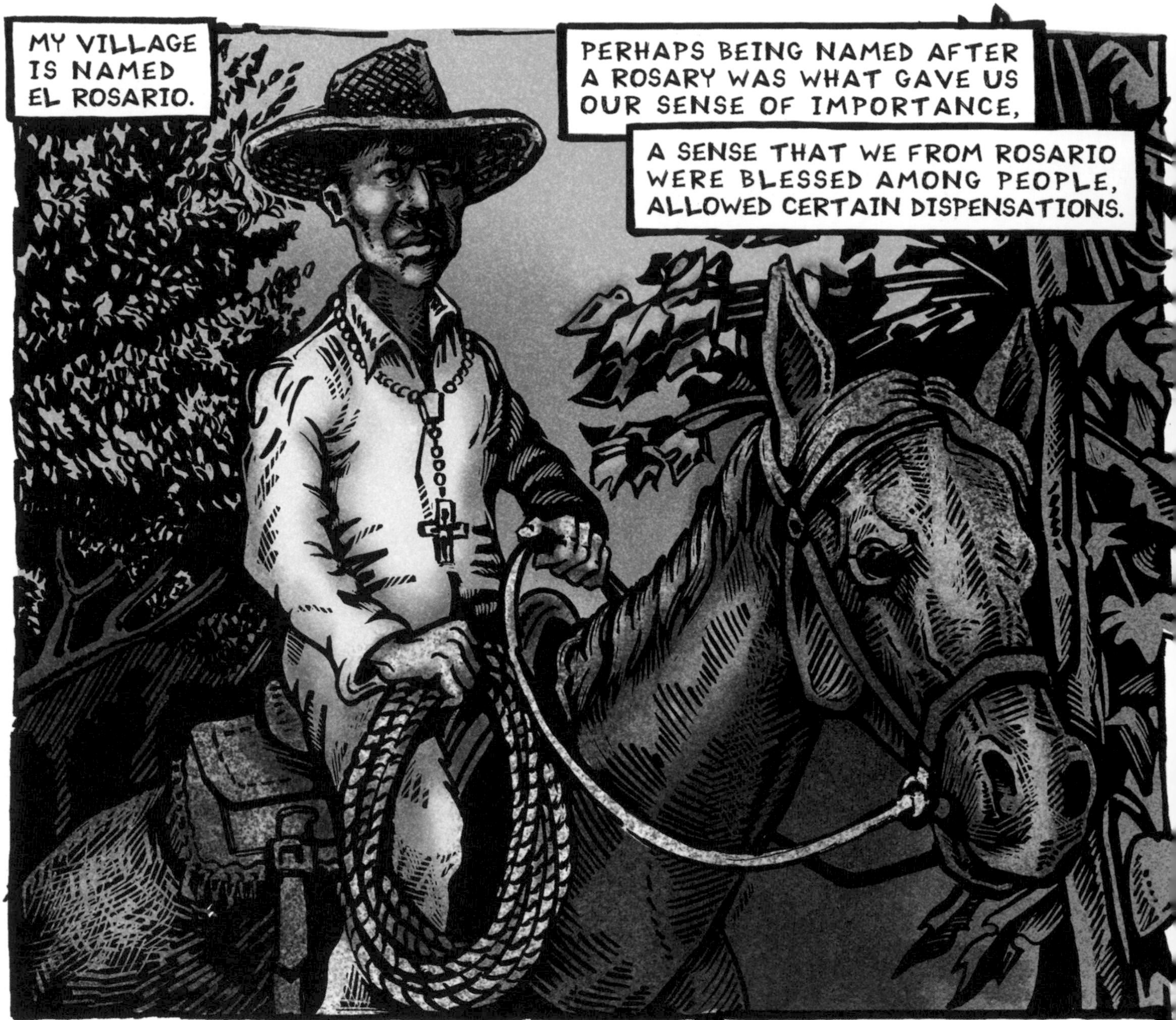
MY VILLAGE IS NAMED EL ROSARIO.
PERHAPS BEING NAMED AFTER A ROSARY WAS WHAT GAVE US OUR SENSE OF IMPORTANCE,
A SENSE THAT WE FROM ROSARIO WERE BLESSED AMONG PEOPLE, ALLOWED CERTAIN DISPENSATIONS.

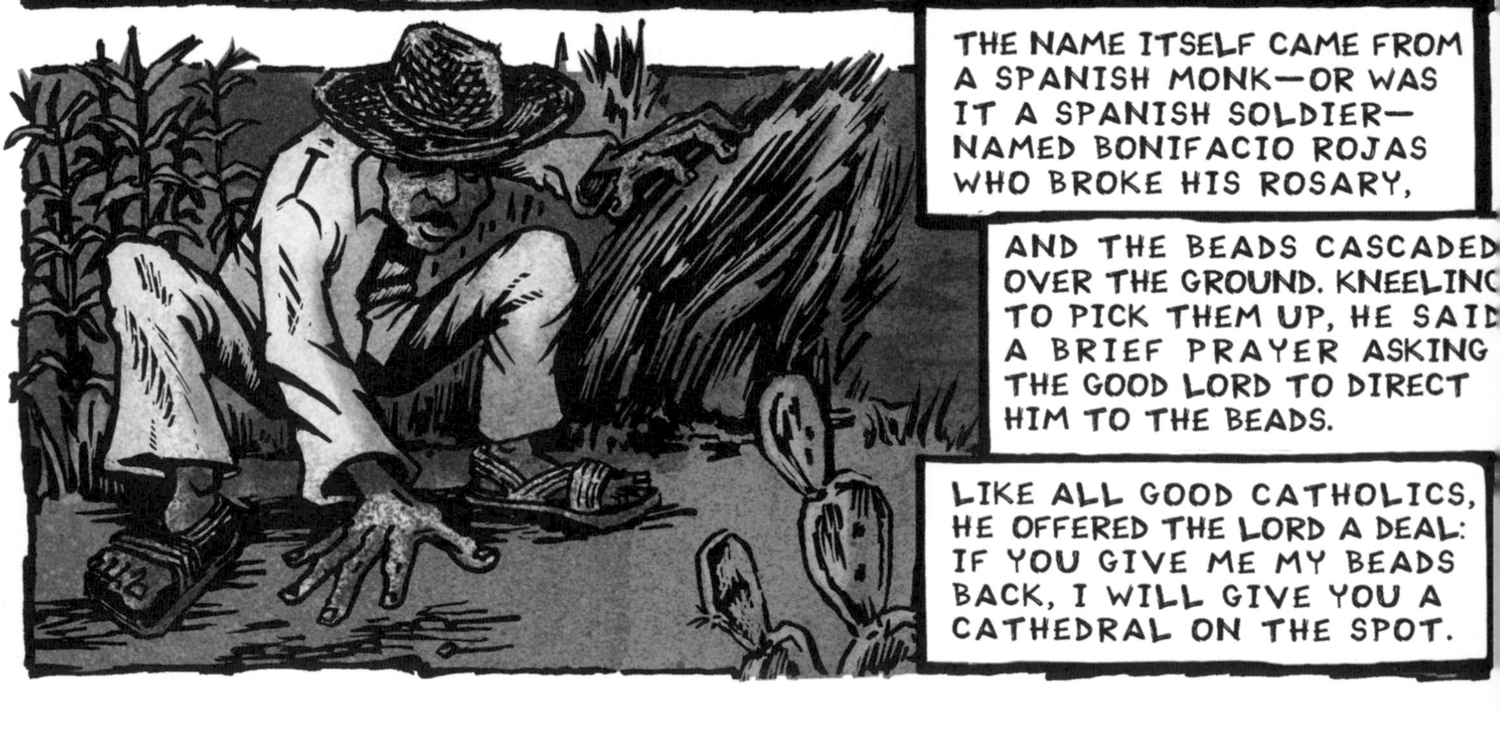
THE NAME ITSELF CAME FROM A SPANISH MONK—OR WAS IT A SPANISH SOLDIER—NAMED BONIFACIO ROJAS WHO BROKE HIS ROSARY,
AND THE BEADS CASCADED OVER THE GROUND. KNEELING TO PICK THEM UP, HE SAID A BRIEF PRAYER ASKING THE GOOD LORD TO DIRECT HIM TO THE BEADS.
LIKE ALL GOOD CATHOLICS, HE OFFERED THE LORD A DEAL: IF YOU GIVE ME MY BEADS BACK, I WILL GIVE YOU A CATHEDRAL ON THE SPOT.

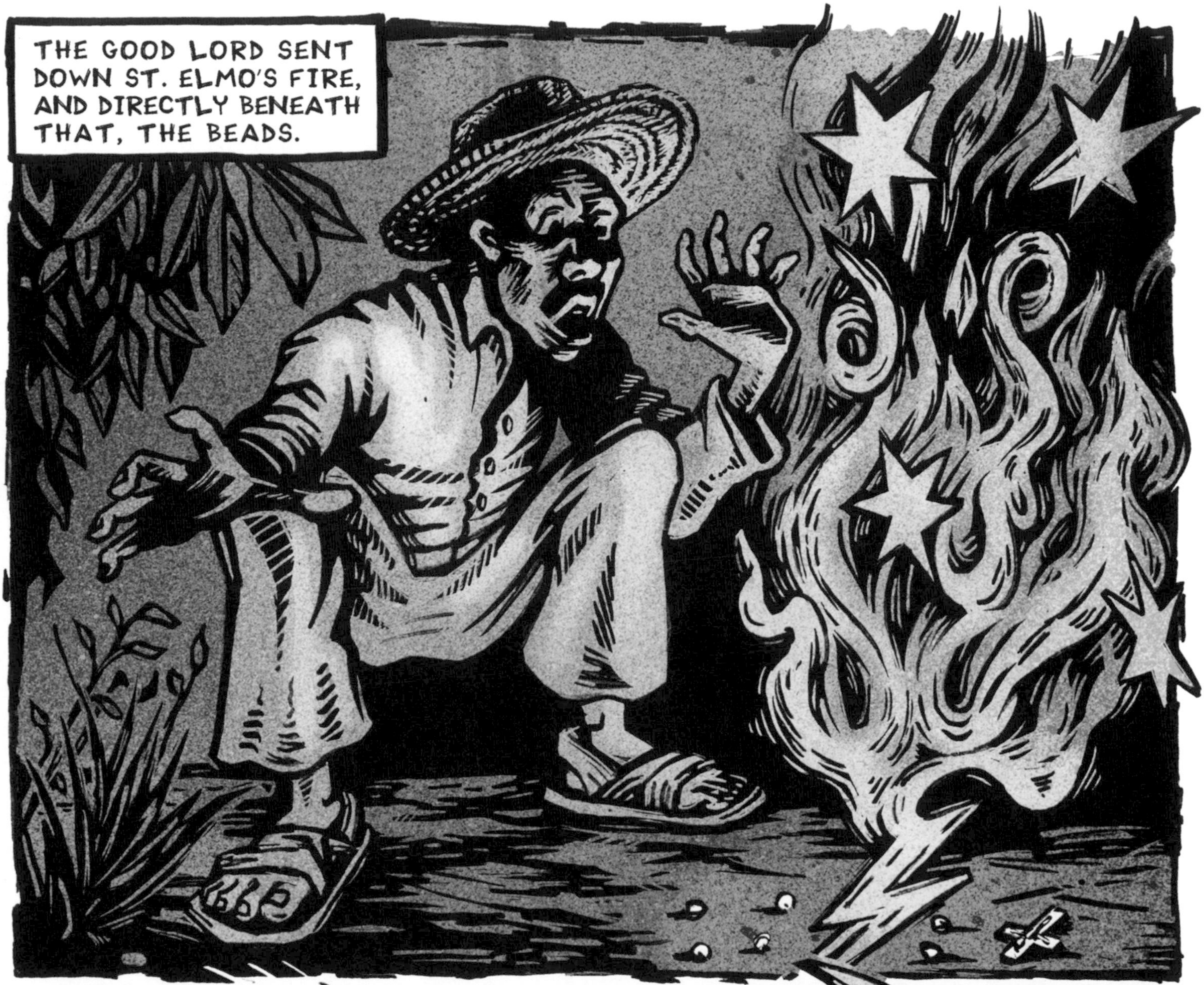
THE GOOD LORD SENT DOWN ST. ELMO'S FIRE, AND DIRECTLY BENEATH THAT, THE BEADS.

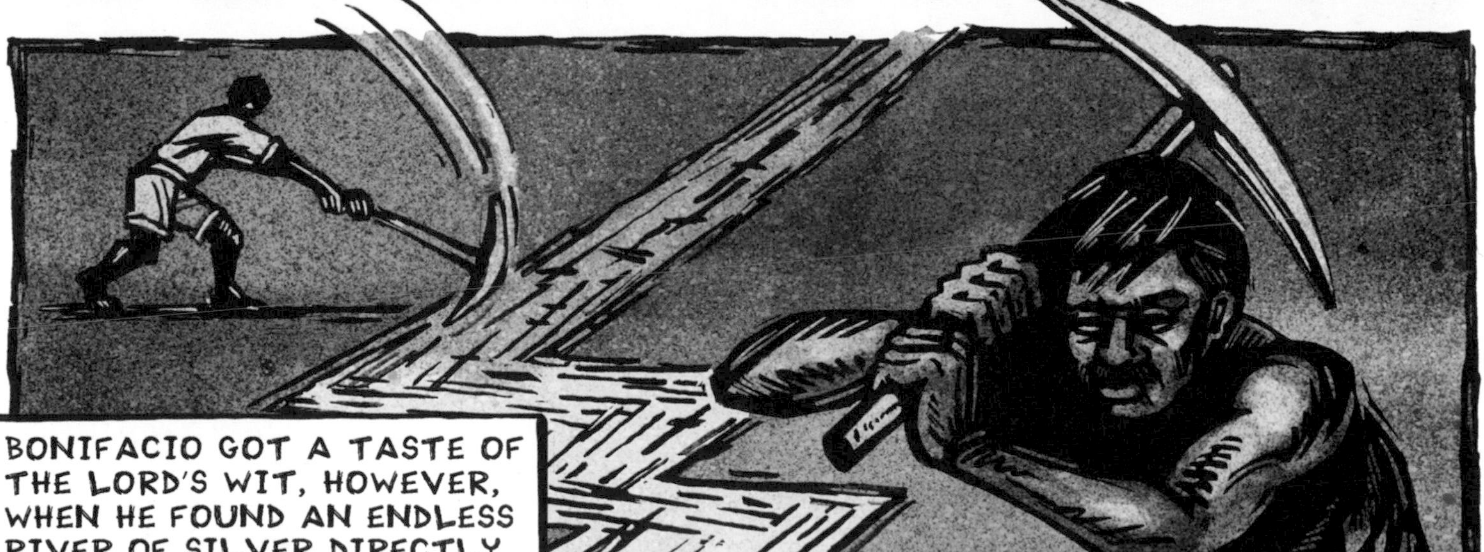
BONIFACIO GOT A TASTE OF THE LORD'S WIT, HOWEVER, WHEN HE FOUND AN ENDLESS RIVER OF SILVER DIRECTLY BENEATH THE BEADS.
IT HAPPENED IN 1655, THE THIRD OF AUGUST. A SATURDAY.

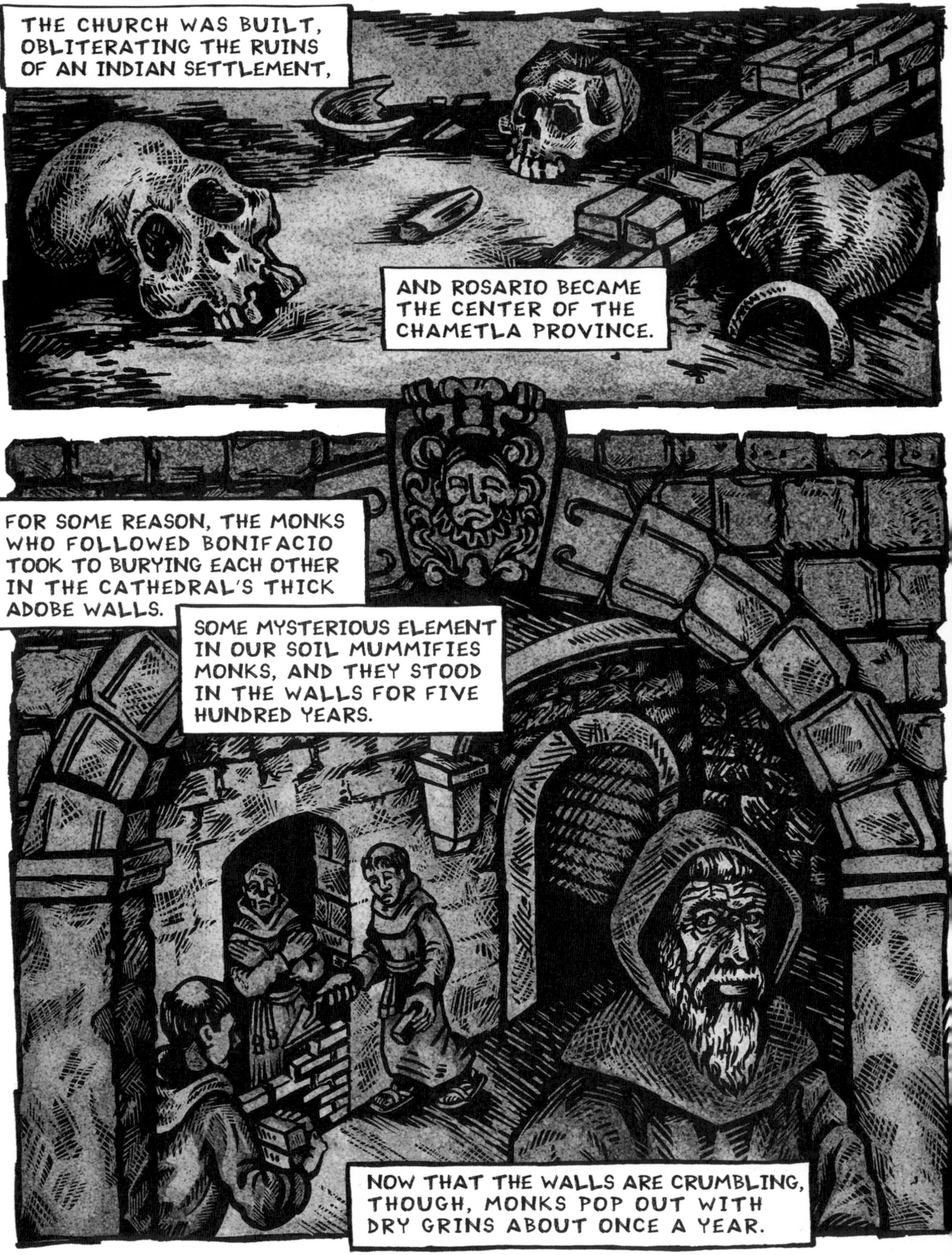
THE CHURCH WAS BUILT, OBLITERATING THE RUINS OF AN INDIAN SETTLEMENT,
AND ROSARIO BECAME THE CENTER OF THE CHAMETLA PROVINCE.
FOR SOME REASON, THE MONKS WHO FOLLOWED BONIFACIO TOOK TO BURYING EACH OTHER IN THE CATHEDRAL'S THICK ADOBE WALLS.
SOME MYSTERIOUS ELEMENT IN OUR SOIL MUMMIFIES MONKS, AND THEY STOOD IN THE WALLS FOR FIVE HUNDRED YEARS.
NOW THAT THE WALLS ARE CRUMBLING, THOUGH, MONKS POP OUT WITH DRY GRINS ABOUT ONCE A YEAR.

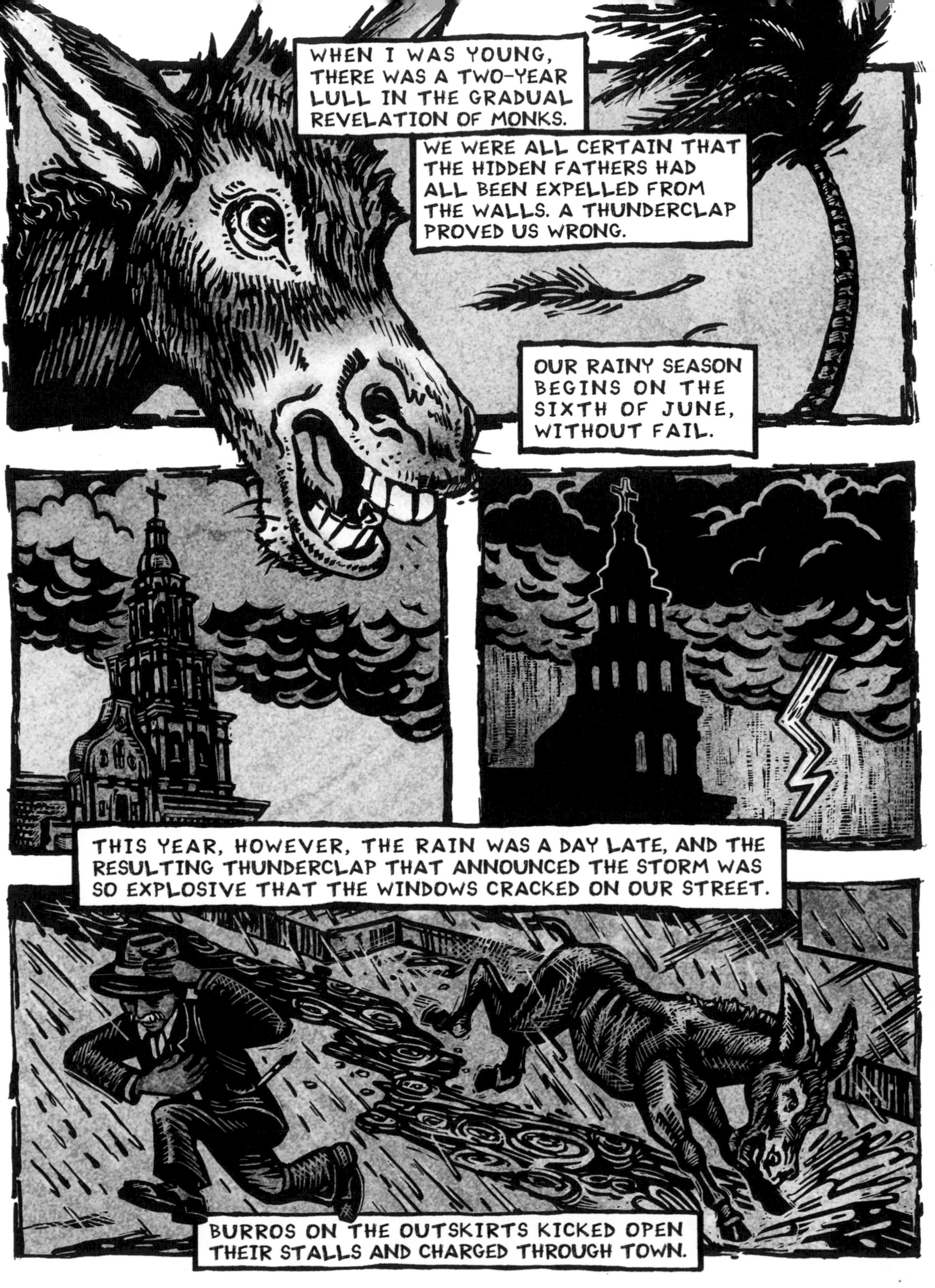
WHEN I WAS YOUNG, THERE WAS A TWO-YEAR LULL IN THE GRADUAL REVELATION OF MONKS.
WE WERE ALL CERTAIN THAT THE HIDDEN FATHERS HAD ALL BEEN EXPELLED FROM THE WALLS. A THUNDERCLAP PROVED US WRONG.
OUR RAINY SEASON BEGINS ON THE SIXTH OF JUNE, WITHOUT FAIL.
THIS YEAR, HOWEVER, THE RAIN WAS A DAY LATE, AND THE RESULTING THUNDERCLAP THAT ANNOUNCED THE STORM WAS SO EXPLOSIVE THAT THE WINDOWS CRACKED ON OUR STREET.
BURROS ON THE OUTSKIRTS KICKED OPEN THEIR STALLS AND CHARGED THROUGH TOWN.

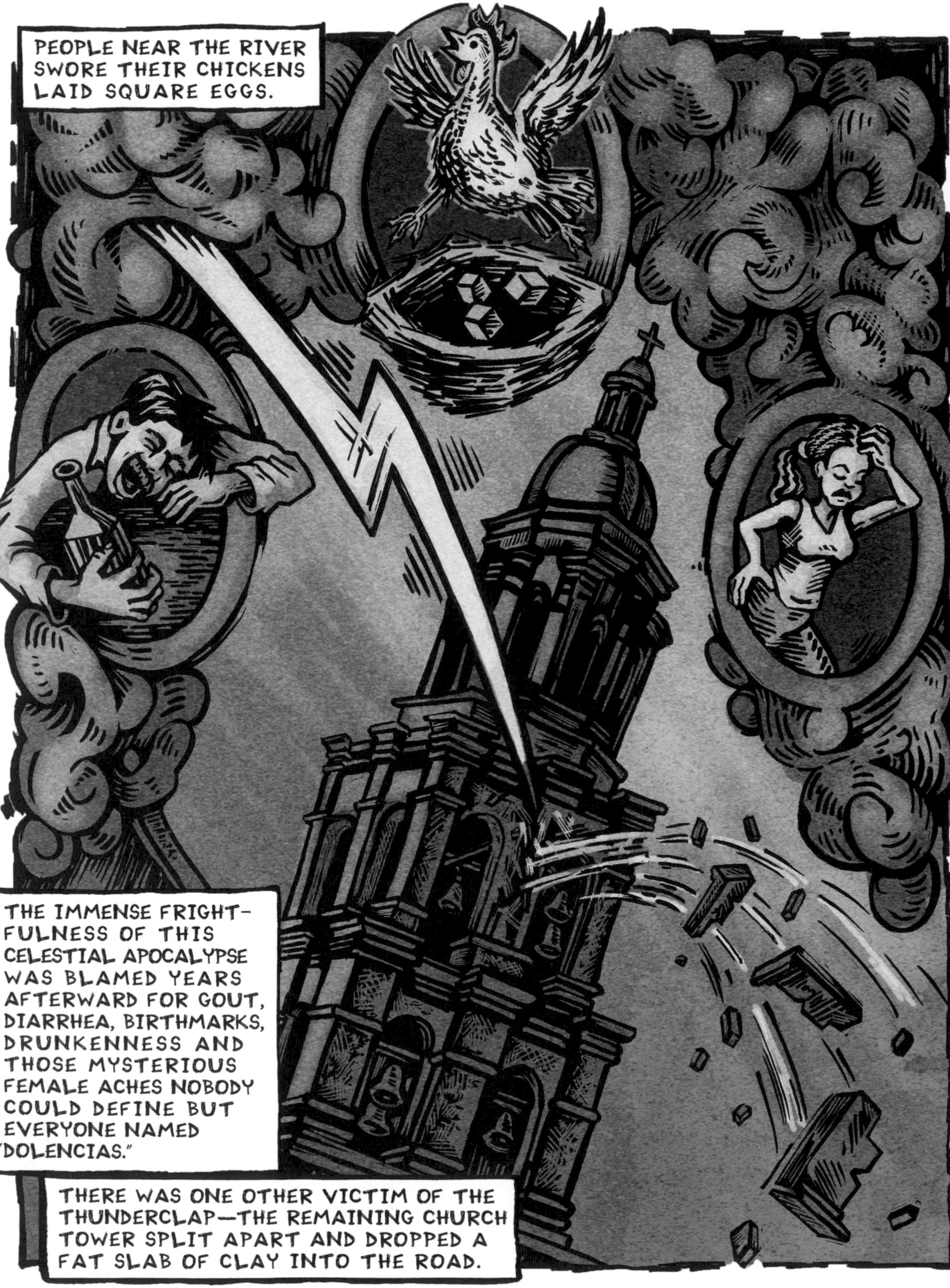
PEOPLE NEAR THE RIVER SWORE THEIR CHICKENS LAID SQUARE EGGS.
THE IMMENSE FRIGHTFULNESS OF THIS CELESTIAL APOCALYPSE WAS BLAMED YEARS AFTERWARD FOR GOUT, DIARRHEA, BIRTHMARKS, DRUNKENNESS AND THOSE MYSTERIOUS FEMALE ACHES NOBODY COULD DEFINE BUT EVERYONE NAMED "DOLENCIAS."
THERE WAS ONE OTHER VICTIM OF THE THUNDERCLAP—THE REMAINING CHURCH TOWER SPLIT APART AND DROPPED A FAT SLAB OF CLAY INTO THE ROAD.

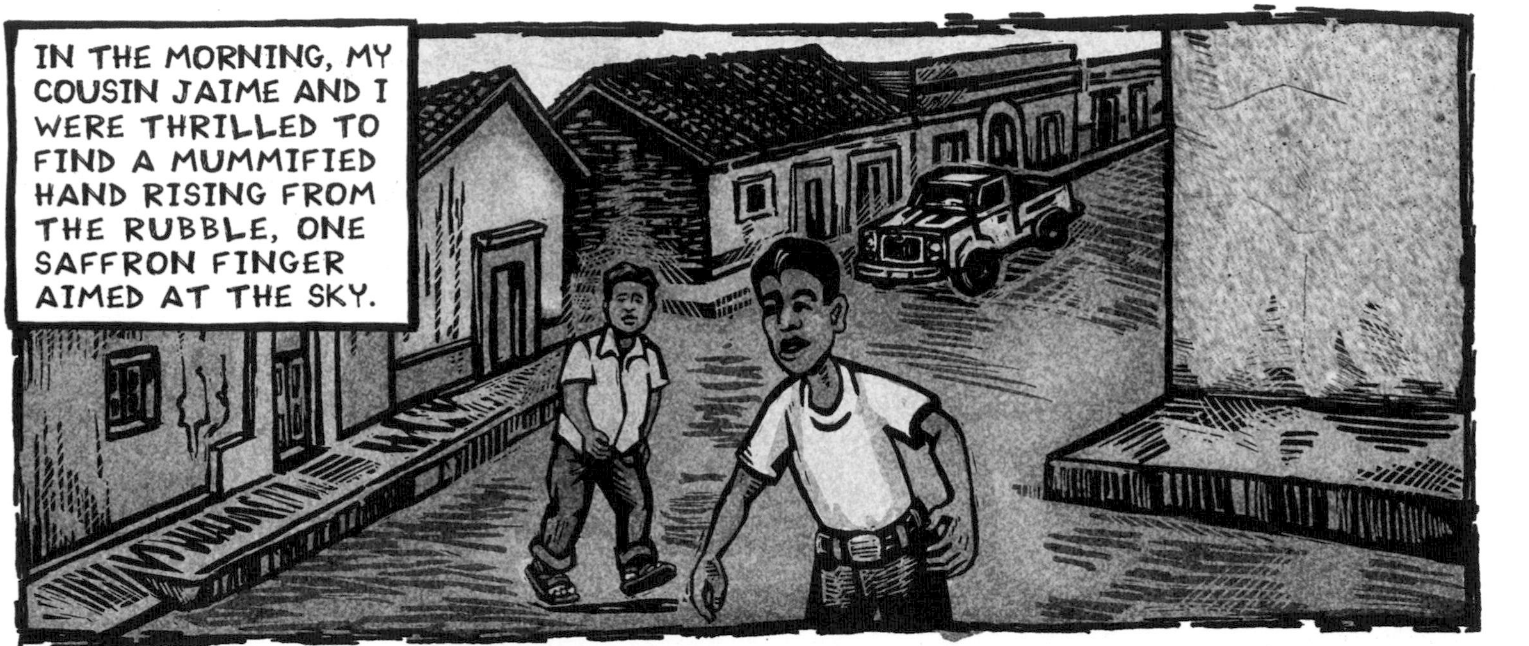
IN THE MORNING, MY COUSIN JAIME AND I WERE THRILLED TO FIND A MUMMIFIED HAND RISING FROM THE RUBBLE, ONE SAFFRON FINGER AIMED AT THE SKY.

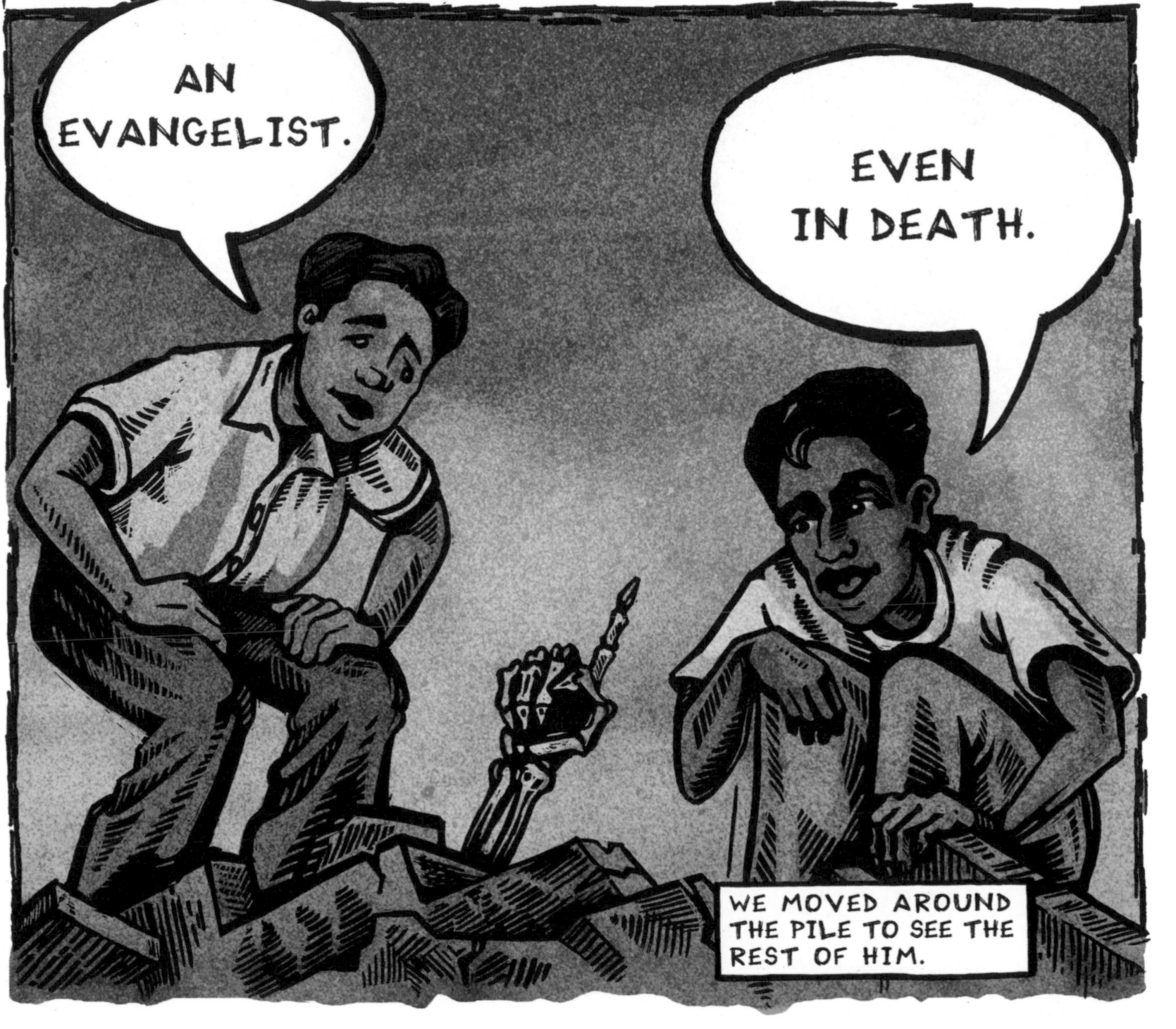
AN EVANGELIST.
EVEN IN DEATH.
WE MOVED AROUND THE PILE TO SEE THE REST OF HIM.

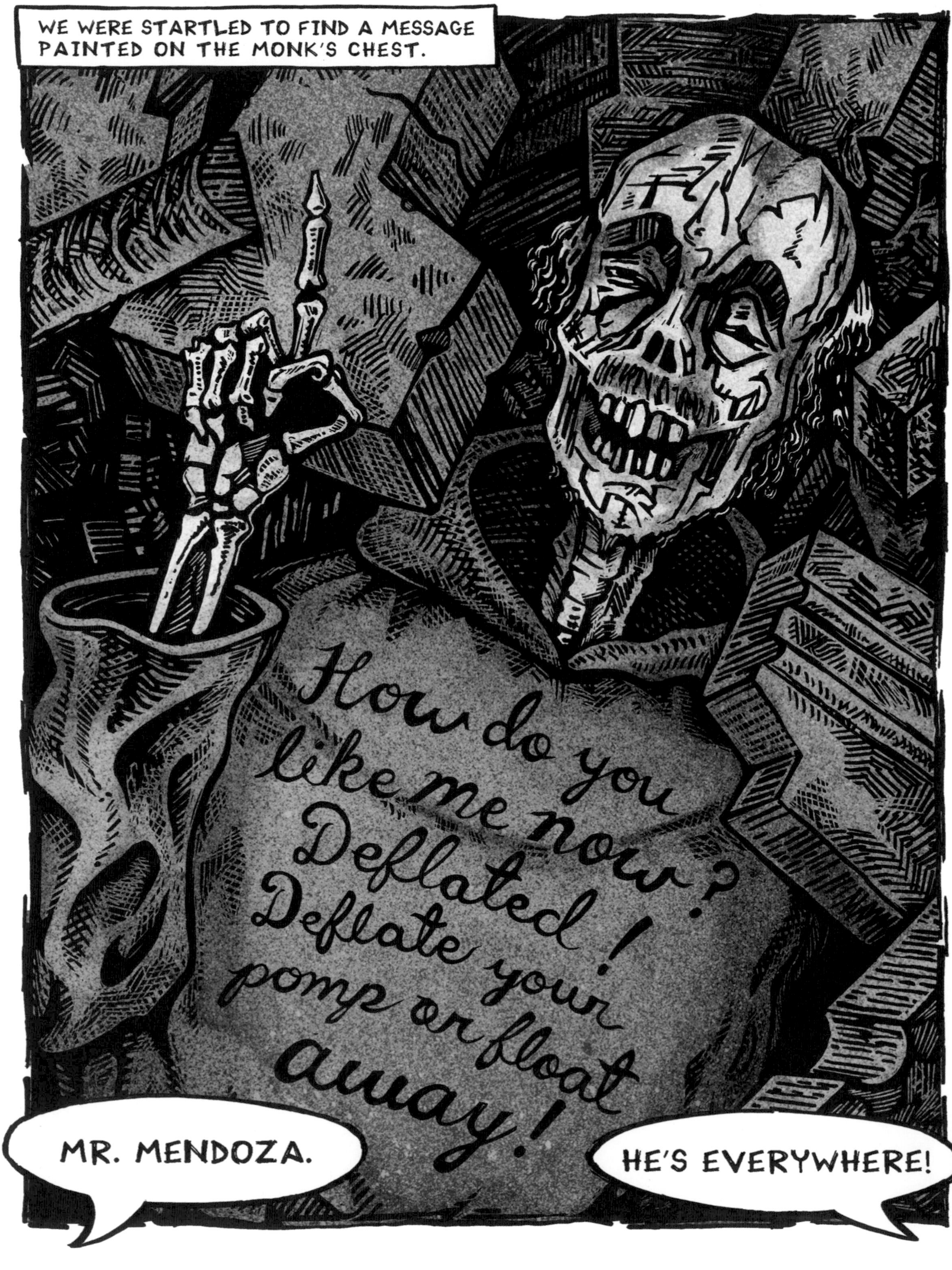
WE WERE STARTLED TO FIND A MESSAGE PAINTED ON THE MONK'S CHEST.
How do you like me now? Deflated! Deflate your pomp or float away!
MR. MENDOZA.
HE'S EVERYWHERE!

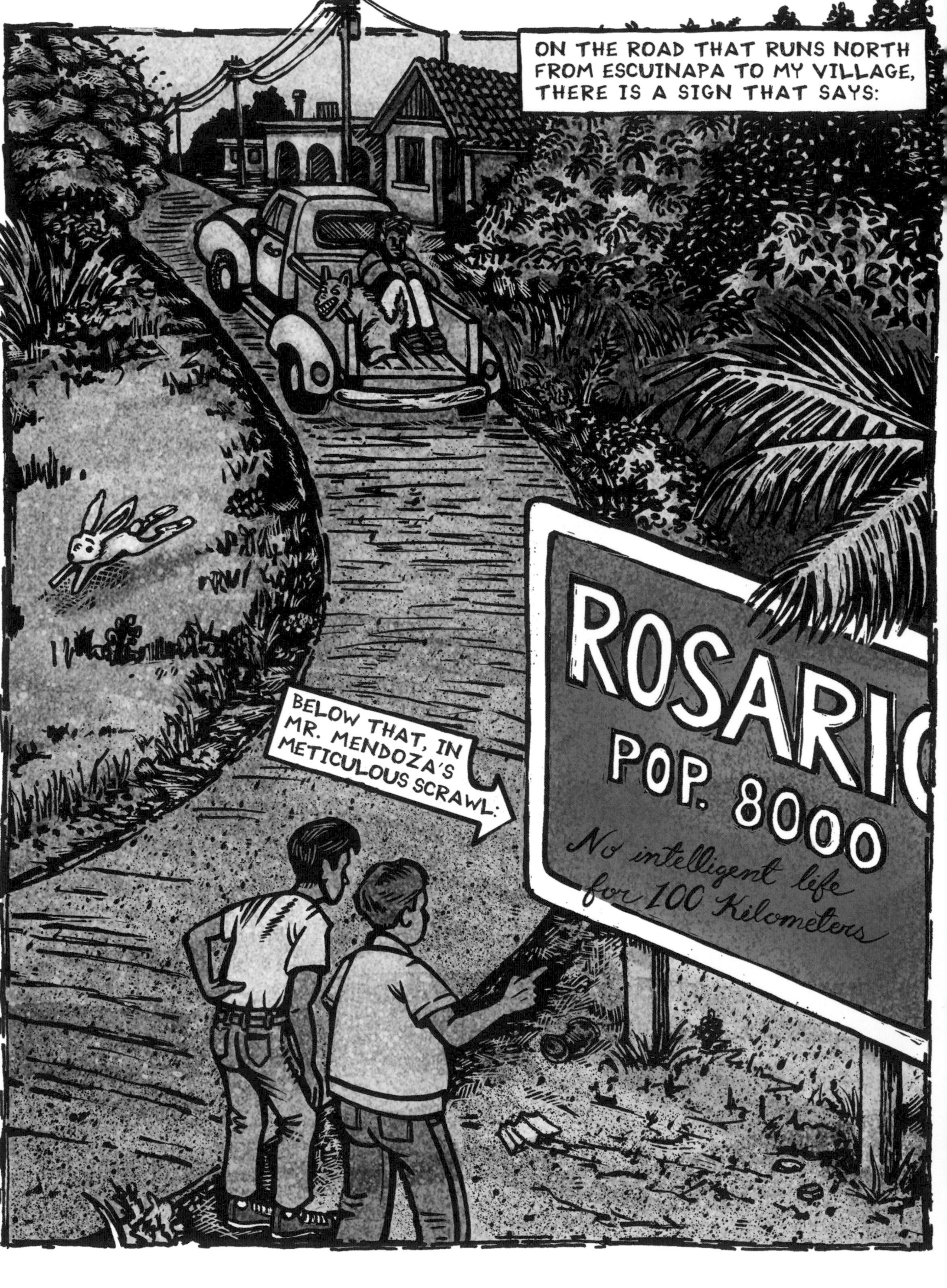
ON THE ROAD THAT RUNS NORTH FROM ESCUINAPA TO MY VILLAGE, THERE IS A SIGN THAT SAYS:
ROSARIO
POP. 8000
BELOW THAT, IN MR. MENDOZA'S METICULOUS SCRAWL:
No intelligent life for 100 Kilometers

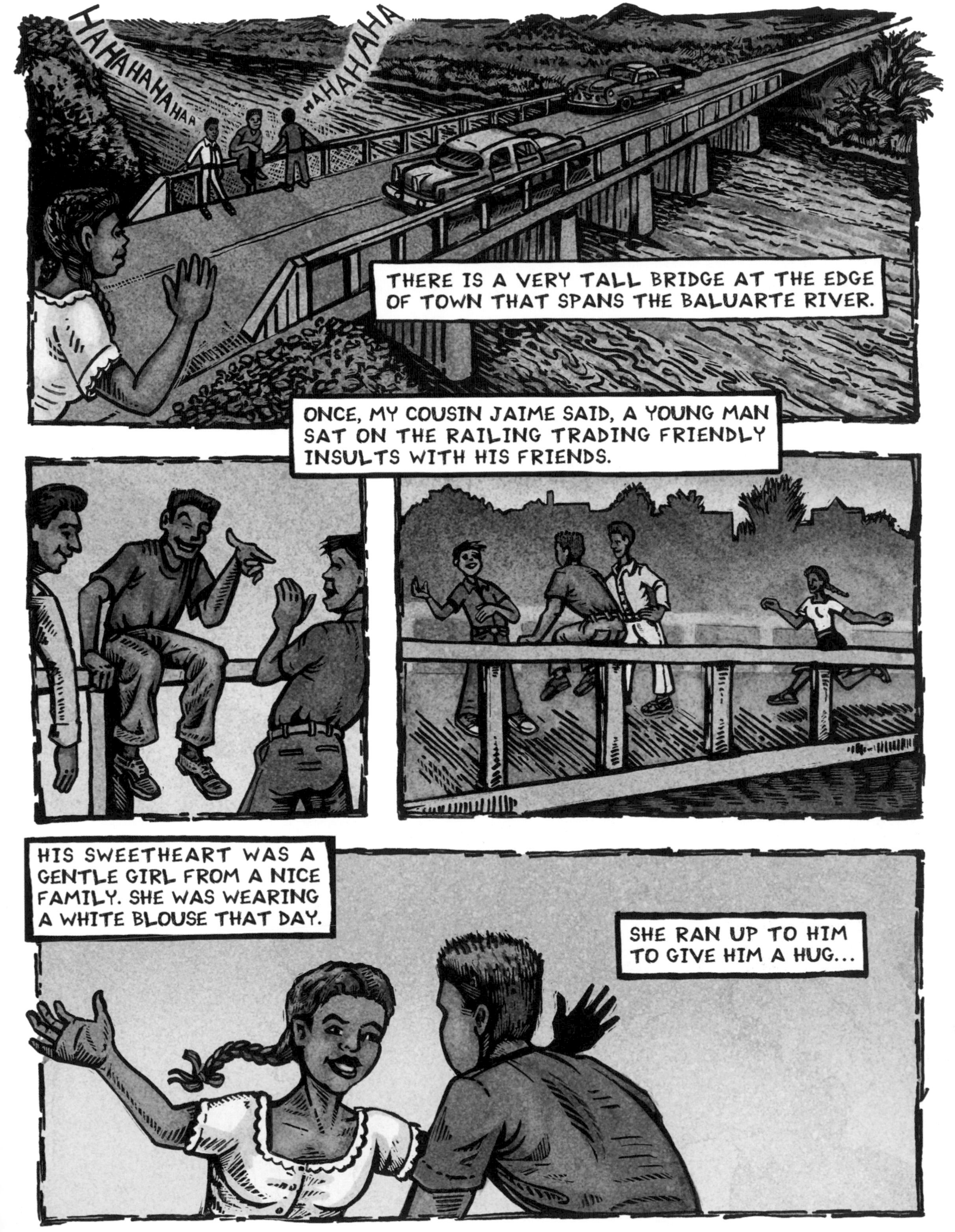
HAHAHAHAHAHAHAA
HAHAHAHAHA
THERE IS A VERY TALL BRIDGE AT THE EDGE OF TOWN THAT SPANS THE BALUARTE RIVER.
ONCE, MY COUSIN JAIME SAID, A YOUNG MAN SAT ON THE RAILING TRADING FRIENDLY INSULTS WITH HIS FRIENDS.
HIS SWEETHEART WAS A GENTLE GIRL FROM A NICE FAMILY. SHE WAS WEARING A WHITE BLOUSE THAT DAY.
SHE RAN UP TO HIM TO GIVE HIM A HUG...

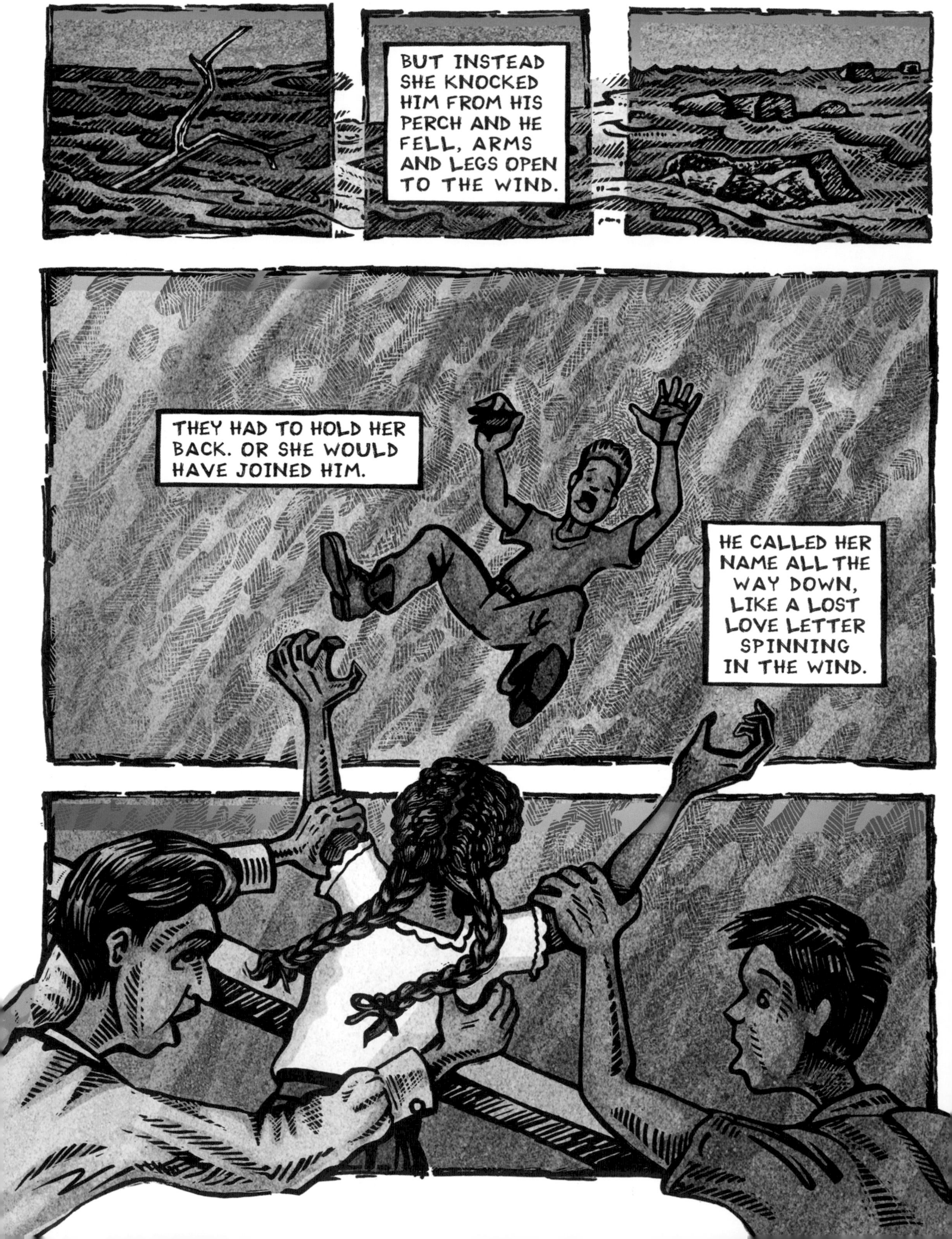
BUT INSTEAD SHE KNOCKED HIM FROM HIS PERCH AND HE FELL, ARMS AND LEGS OPEN TO THE WIND.
THEY HAD TO HOLD HER BACK. OR SHE WOULD HAVE JOINED HIM.
HE CALLED HER NAME ALL THE WAY DOWN, LIKE A LOST LOVE LETTER SPINNING IN THE WIND.

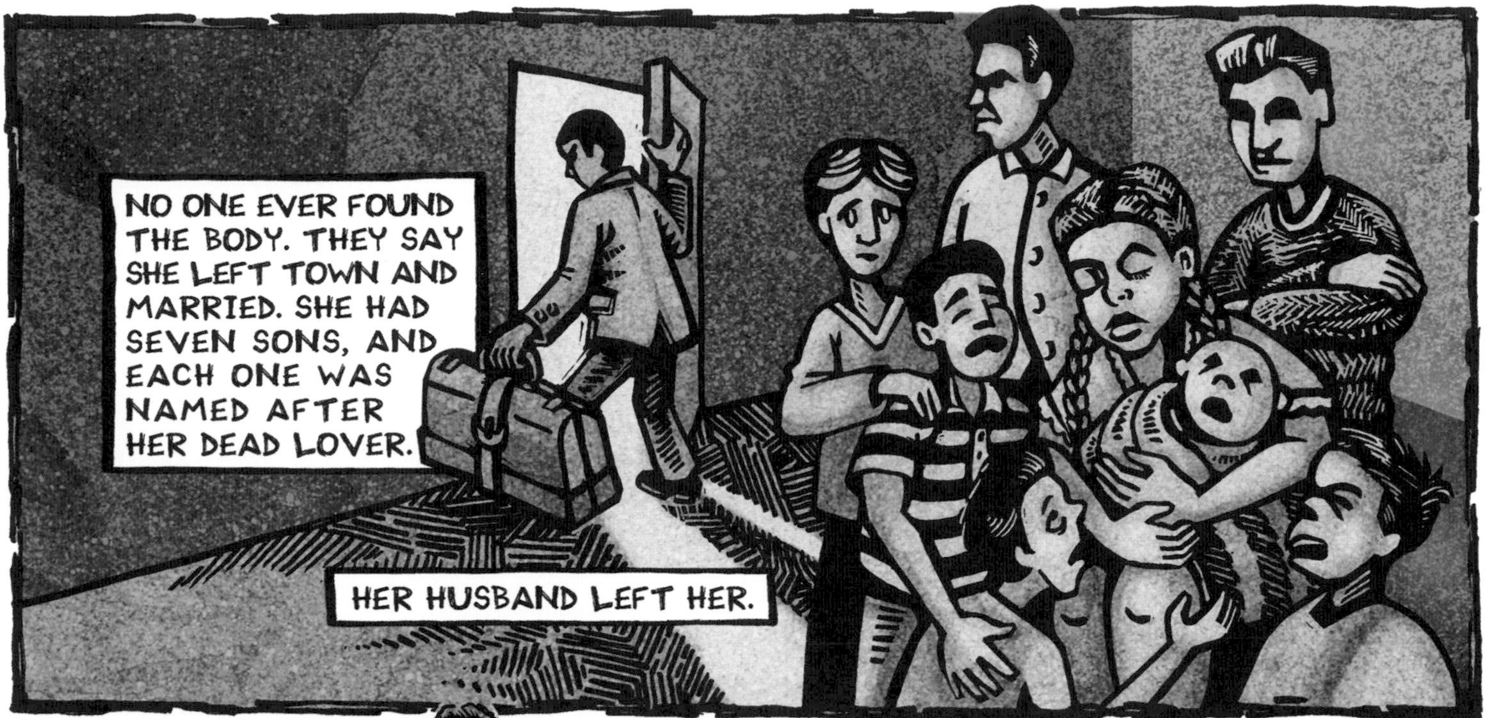
NO ONE EVER FOUND THE BODY. THEY SAY SHE LEFT TOWN AND MARRIED. SHE HAD SEVEN SONS, AND EACH ONE WAS NAMED AFTER HER DEAD LOVER.
HER HUSBAND LEFT HER.

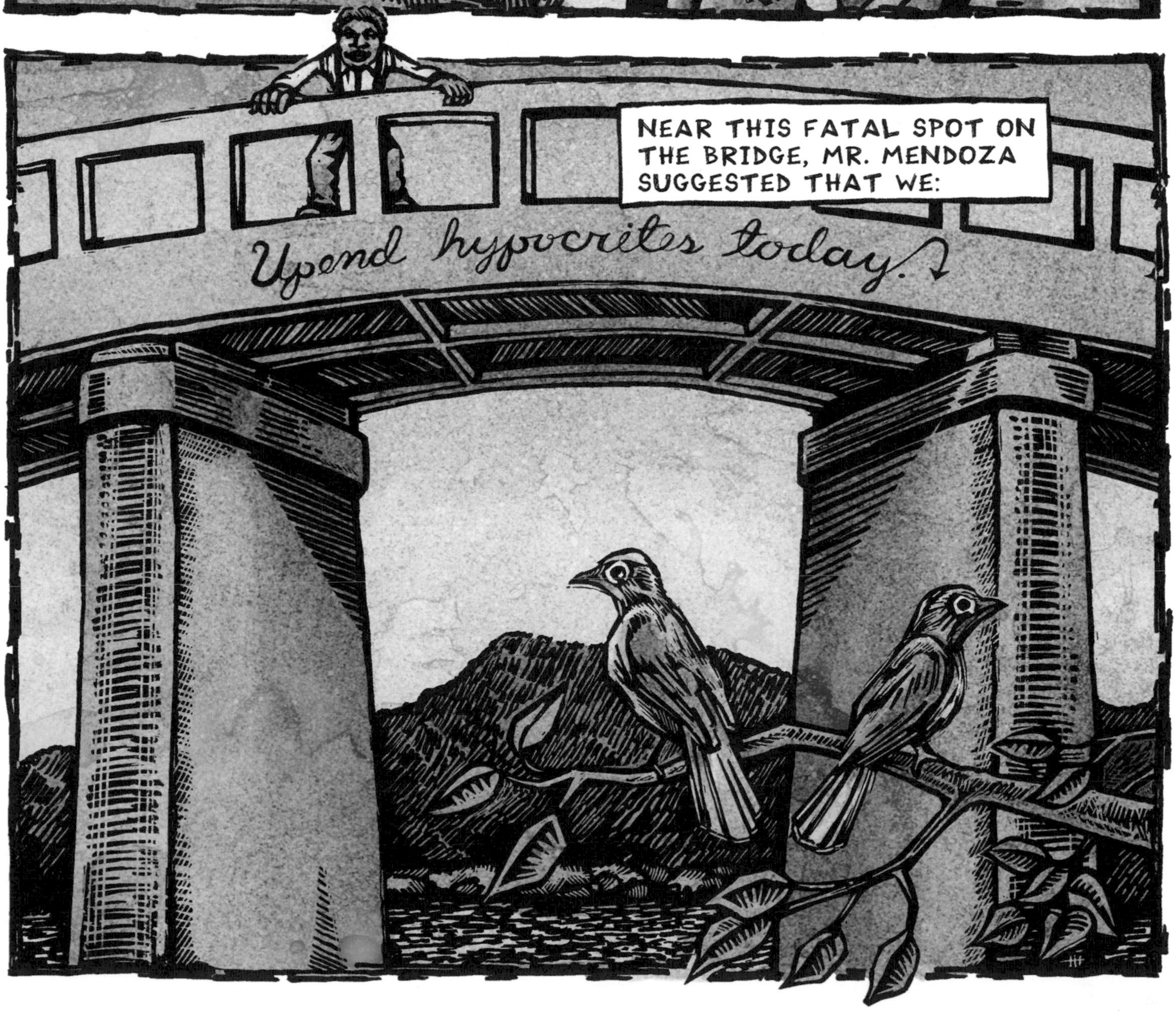
NEAR THIS FATAL SPOT ON THE BRIDGE, MR. MENDOZA SUGGESTED THAT WE:
Upend hypocrites today.

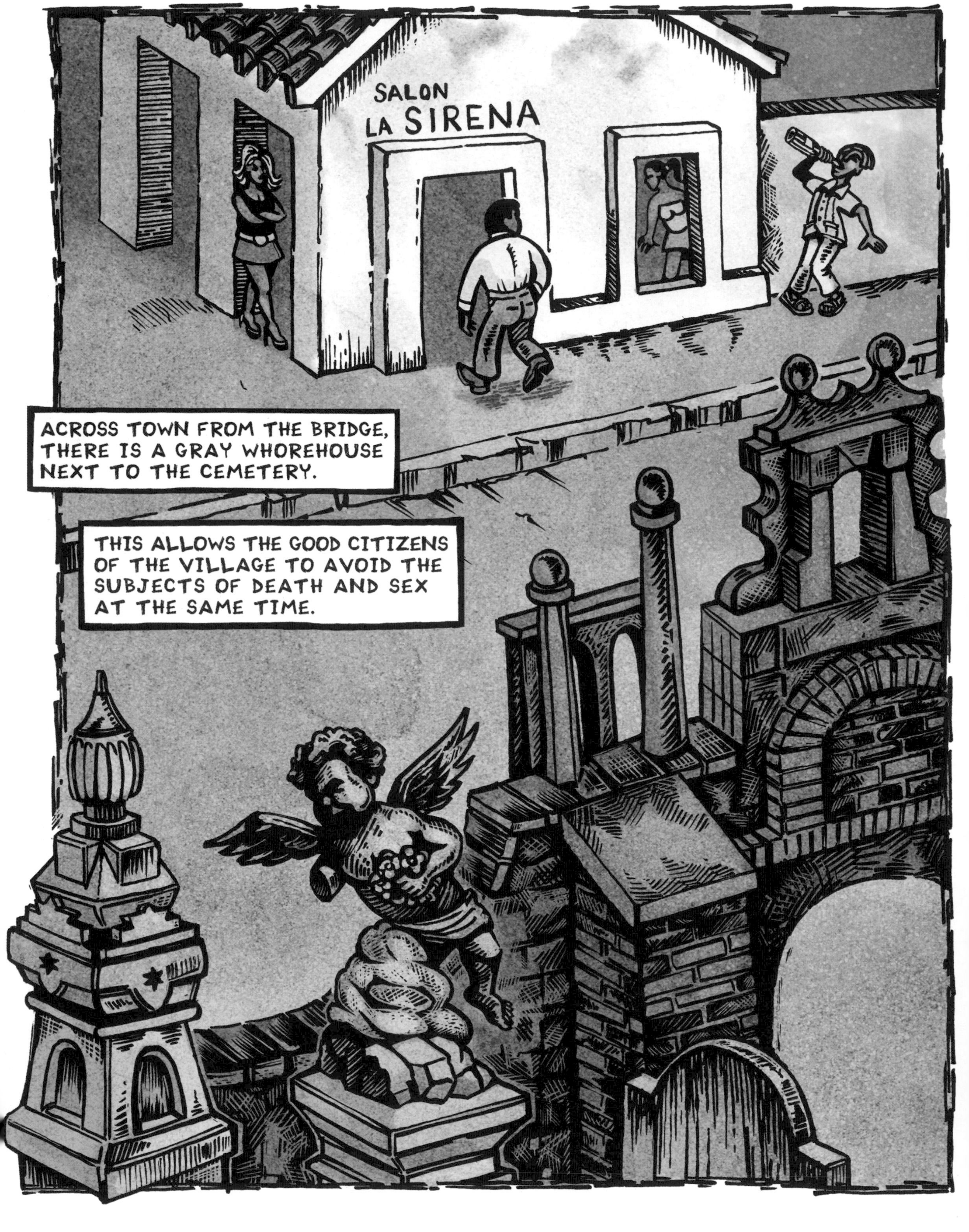
SALON
LA SIRENA
ACROSS TOWN FROM THE BRIDGE, THERE IS A GRAY WHOREHOUSE NEXT TO THE CEMETERY.
THIS ALLOWS THE GOOD CITIZENS OF THE VILLAGE TO AVOID THE SUBJECTS OF DEATH AND SEX AT THE SAME TIME.

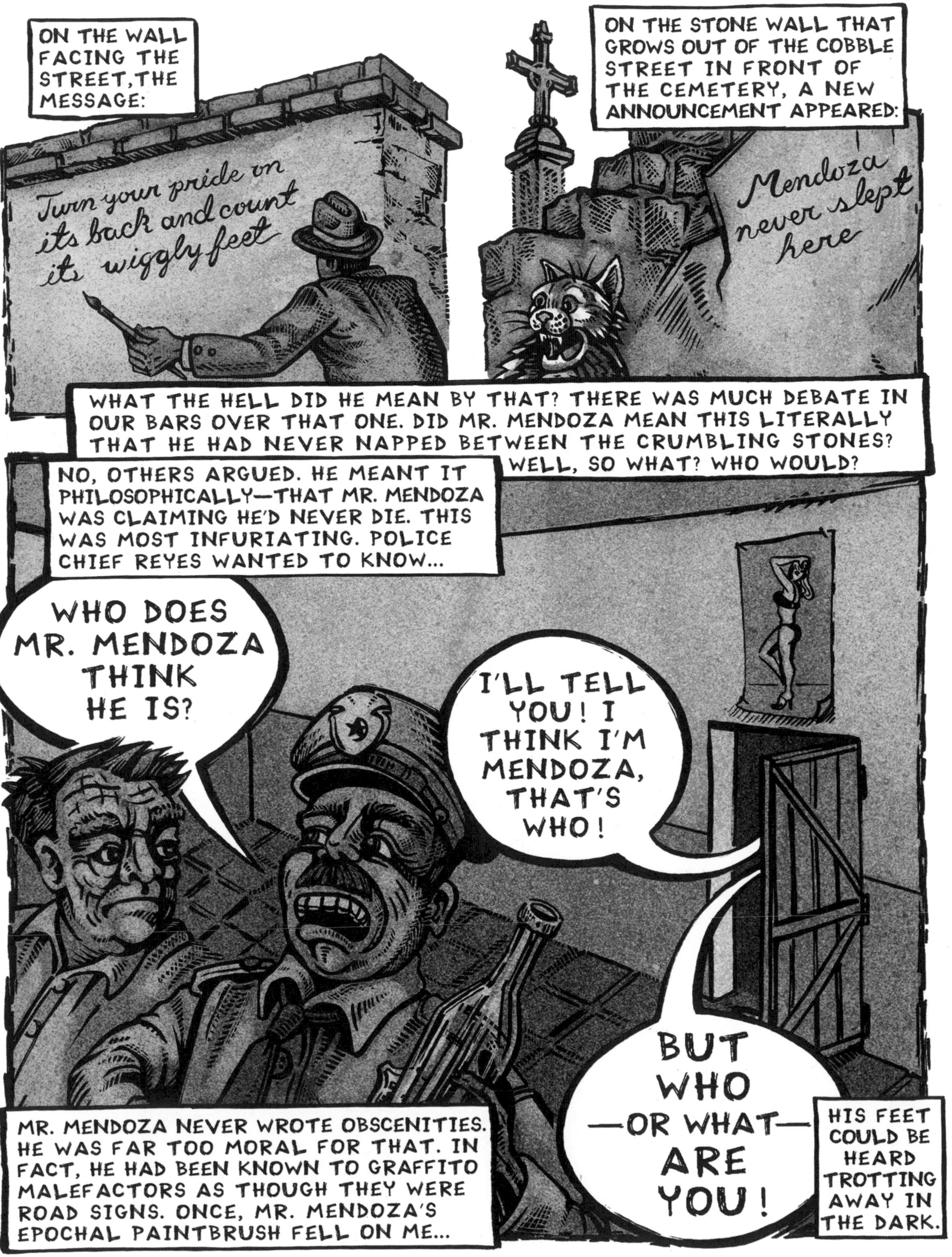
ON THE WALL FACING THE STREET, THE MESSAGE:
Turn your pride on its back and count its wiggly feet
ON THE STONE WALL THAT GROWS OUT OF THE COBBLE STREET IN FRONT OF THE CEMETERY, A NEW ANNOUNCEMENT APPEARED:
Mendoza never slept here
WHAT THE HELL DID HE MEAN BY THAT? THERE WAS MUCH DEBATE IN OUR BARS OVER THAT ONE. DID MR. MENDOZA MEAN THIS LITERALLY THAT HE HAD NEVER NAPPED BETWEEN THE CRUMBLING STONES? WELL, SO WHAT? WHO WOULD?
NO, OTHERS ARGUED. HE MEANT IT PHILOSOPHICALLY—THAT MR. MENDOZA WAS CLAIMING HE'D NEVER DIE. THIS WAS MOST INFURIATING. POLICE CHIEF REYES WANTED TO KNOW...
WHO DOES MR. MENDOZA THINK HE IS?
I'LL TELL YOU! I THINK I'M MENDOZA, THAT'S WHO!
BUT WHO —OR WHAT— ARE YOU!
MR. MENDOZA NEVER WROTE OBSCENITIES. HE WAS FAR TOO MORAL FOR THAT. IN FACT, HE HAD BEEN KNOWN TO GRAFFITO MALEFACTORS AS THOUGH THEY WERE ROAD SIGNS. ONCE, MR. MENDOZA'S EPOCHAL PAINTBRUSH FELL ON ME...
HIS FEET COULD BE HEARD TROTTING AWAY IN THE DARK.

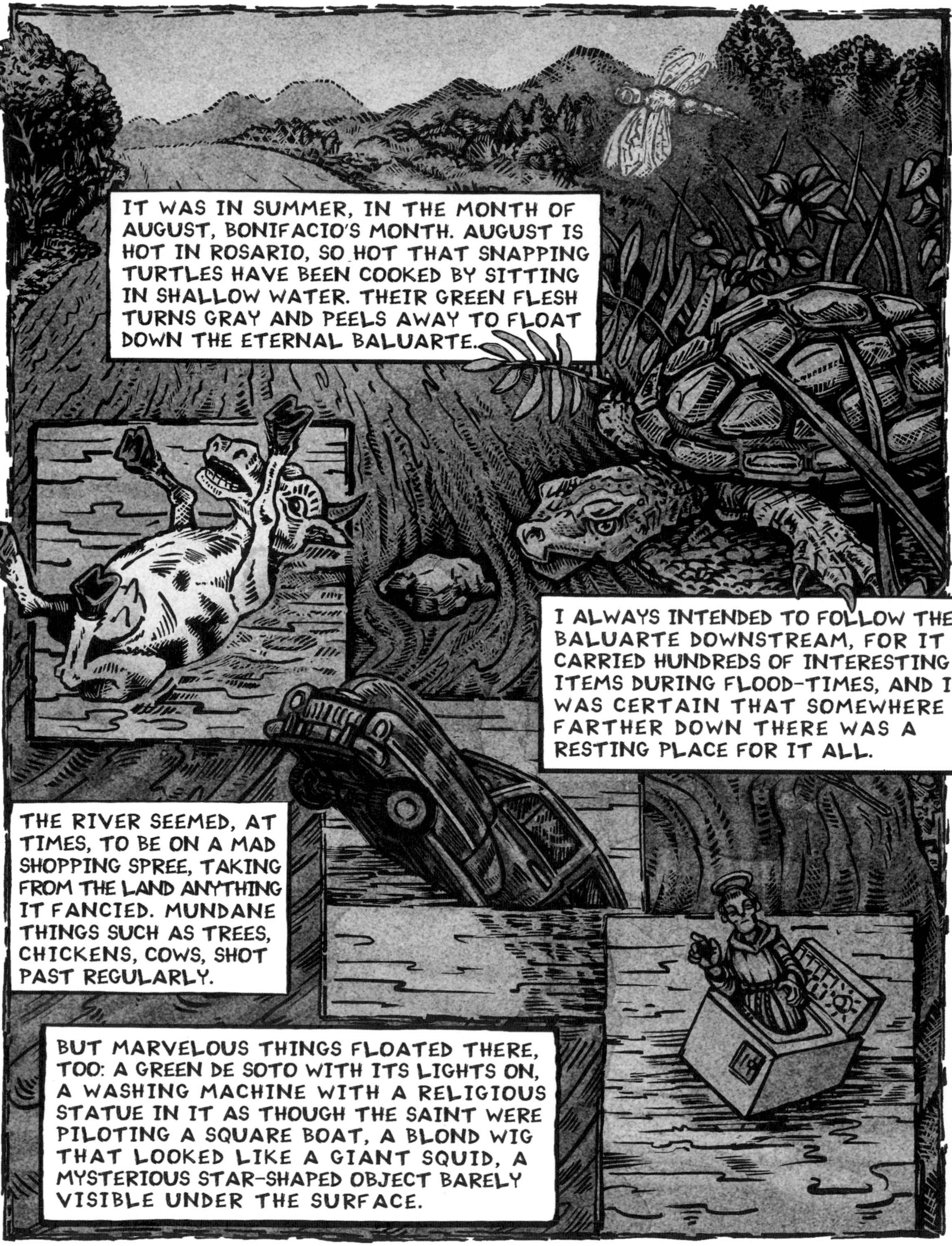
IT WAS IN SUMMER, IN THE MONTH OF AUGUST, BONIFACIO'S MONTH. AUGUST IS HOT IN ROSARIO, SO HOT THAT SNAPPING TURTLES HAVE BEEN COOKED BY SITTING IN SHALLOW WATER. THEIR GREEN FLESH TURNS GRAY AND PEELS AWAY TO FLOAT DOWN THE ETERNAL BALUARTE.
I ALWAYS INTENDED TO FOLLOW THE BALUARTE DOWNSTREAM, FOR IT CARRIED HUNDREDS OF INTERESTING ITEMS DURING FLOOD-TIMES, AND I WAS CERTAIN THAT SOMEWHERE FARTHER DOWN THERE WAS A RESTING PLACE FOR IT ALL.
THE RIVER SEEMED, AT TIMES, TO BE ON A MAD SHOPPING SPREE, TAKING FROM THE LAND ANYTHING IT FANCIED. MUNDANE THINGS SUCH AS TREES, CHICKENS, COWS, SHOT PAST REGULARLY.
BUT MARVELOUS THINGS FLOATED THERE, TOO: A GREEN DE SOTO WITH ITS LIGHTS ON, A WASHING MACHINE WITH A RELIGIOUS STATUE IN IT AS THOUGH THE SAINT WERE PILOTING A SQUARE BOAT, A BLOND WIG THAT LOOKED LIKE A GIANT SQUID, A MYSTERIOUS STAR-SHAPED OBJECT BARELY VISIBLE UNDER THE SURFACE.

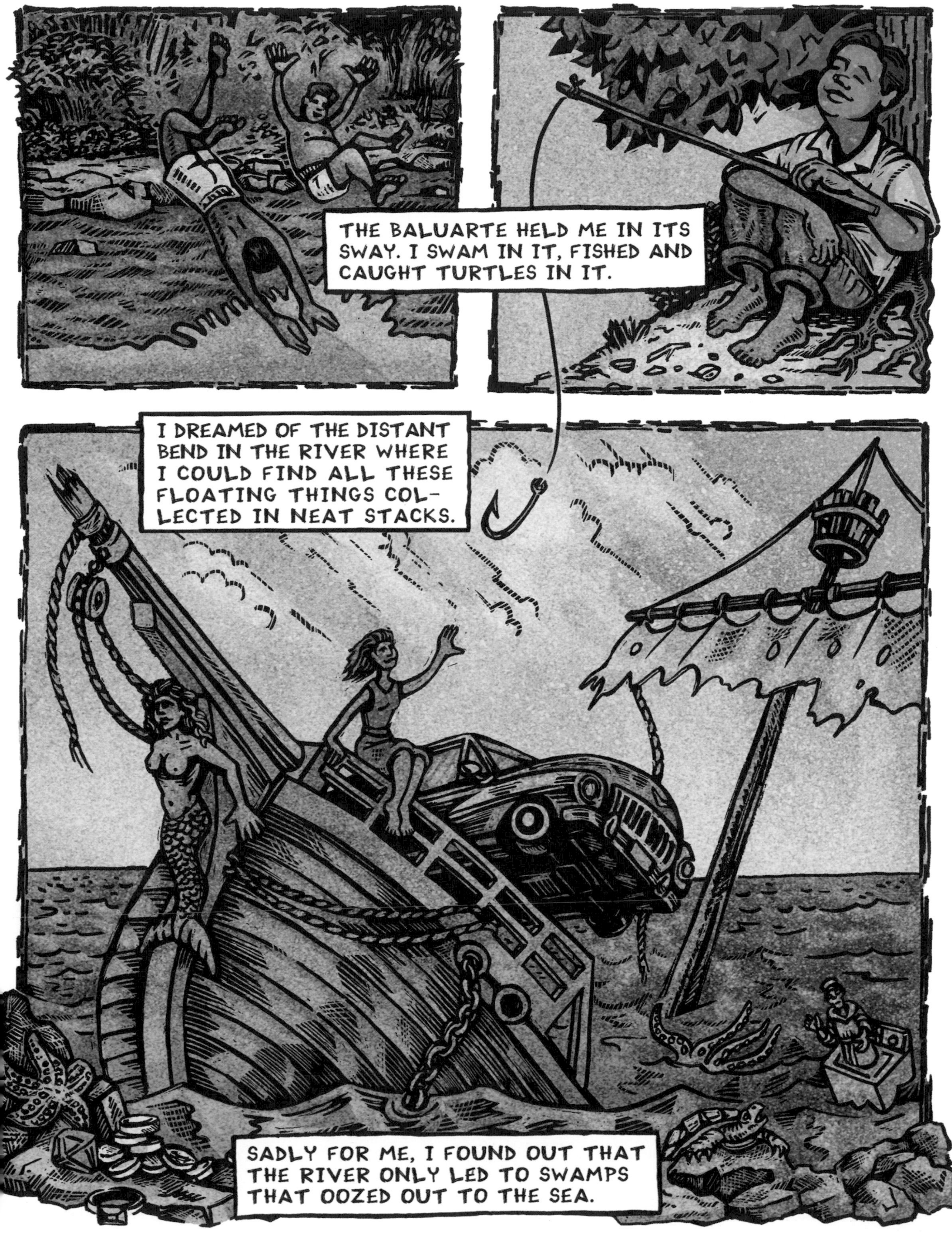
THE BALUARTE HELD ME IN ITS SWAY. I SWAM IN IT, FISHED AND CAUGHT TURTLES IN IT.
I DREAMED OF THE DISTANT BEND IN THE RIVER WHERE I COULD FIND ALL THESE FLOATING THINGS COL-LECTED IN NEAT STACKS.
SADLY FOR ME, I FOUND OUT THAT THE RIVER ONLY LED TO SWAMPS THAT OOZED OUT TO THE SEA.

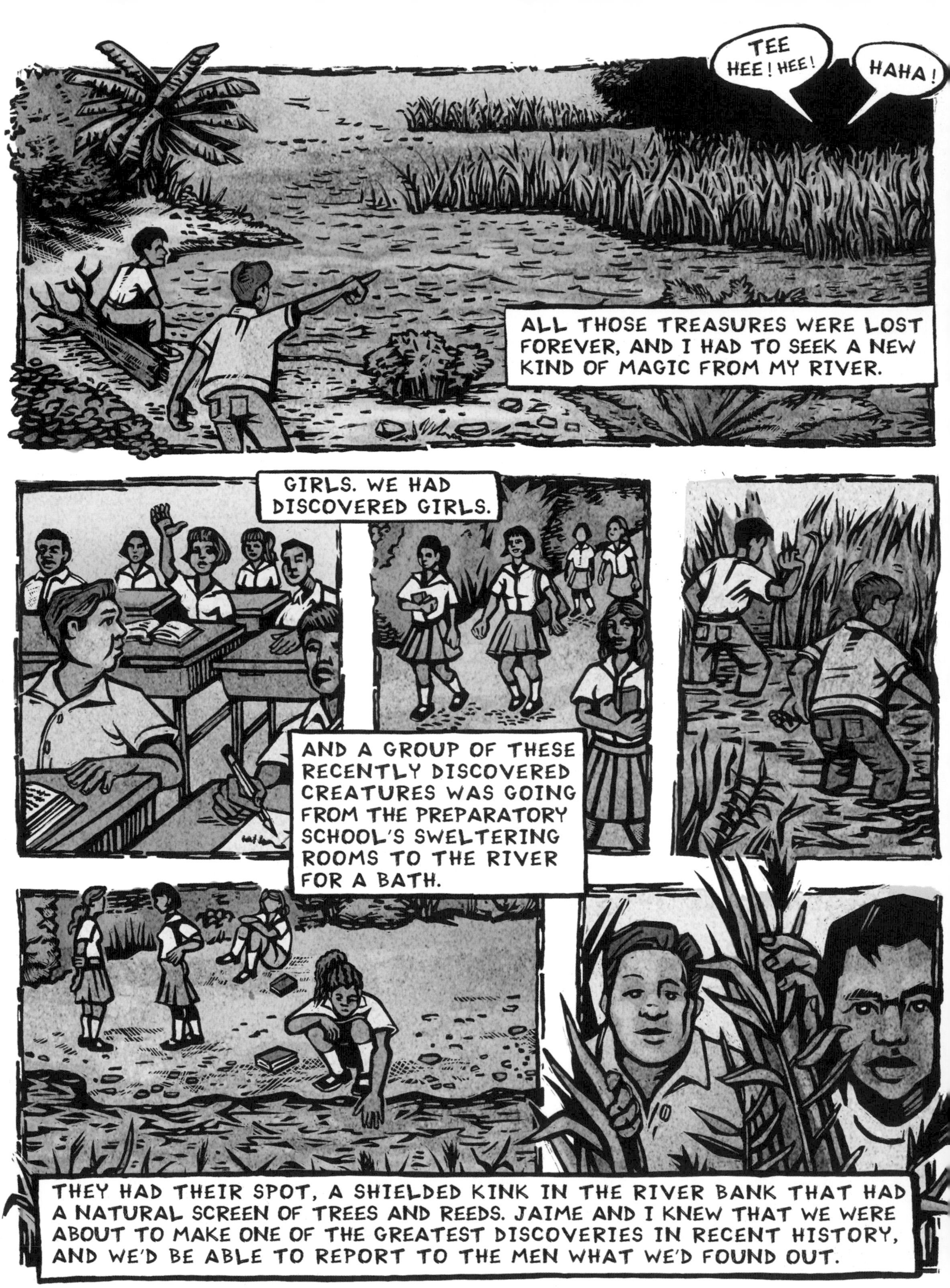
TEE HEE! HEE!
HAHA!
ALL THOSE TREASURES WERE LOST FOREVER, AND I HAD TO SEEK A NEW KIND OF MAGIC FROM MY RIVER.
GIRLS. WE HAD DISCOVERED GIRLS.
AND A GROUP OF THESE RECENTLY DISCOVERED CREATURES WAS GOING FROM THE PREPARATORY SCHOOL'S SWELTERING ROOMS TO THE RIVER FOR A BATH.
THEY HAD THEIR SPOT, A SHIELDED KINK IN THE RIVER BANK THAT HAD A NATURAL SCREEN OF TREES AND REEDS. JAIME AND I KNEW THAT WE WERE ABOUT TO MAKE ONE OF THE GREATEST DISCOVERIES IN RECENT HISTORY, AND WE'D BE ABLE TO REPORT TO THE MEN WHAT WE'D FOUND OUT.

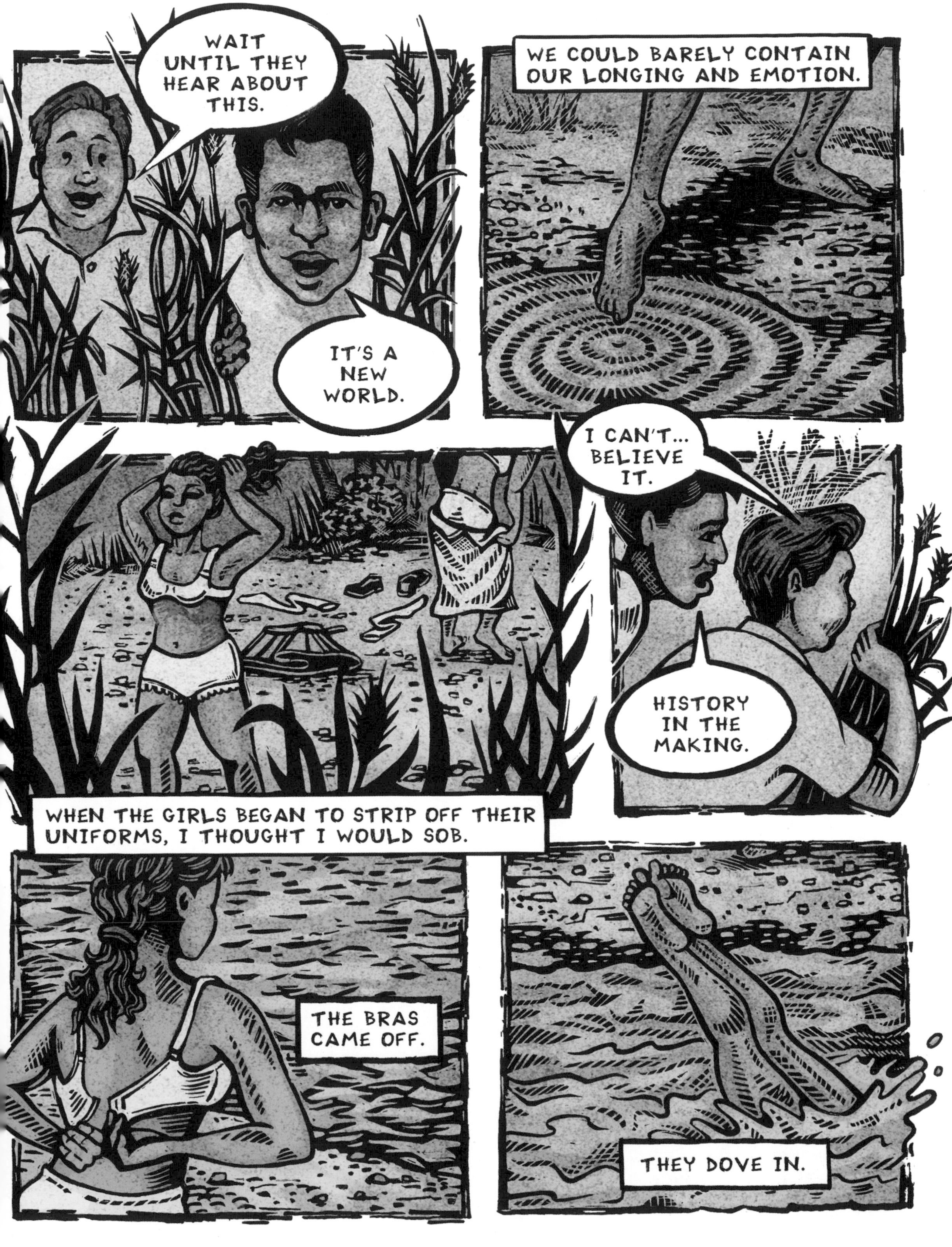
WAIT UNTIL THEY HEAR ABOUT THIS.
IT'S A NEW WORLD.
WE COULD BARELY CONTAIN OUR LONGING AND EMOTION.
I CAN'T... BELIEVE IT.
HISTORY IN THE MAKING.
WHEN THE GIRLS BEGAN TO STRIP OFF THEIR UNIFORMS, I THOUGHT I WOULD SOB.
THE BRAS CAME OFF.
THEY DOVE IN.

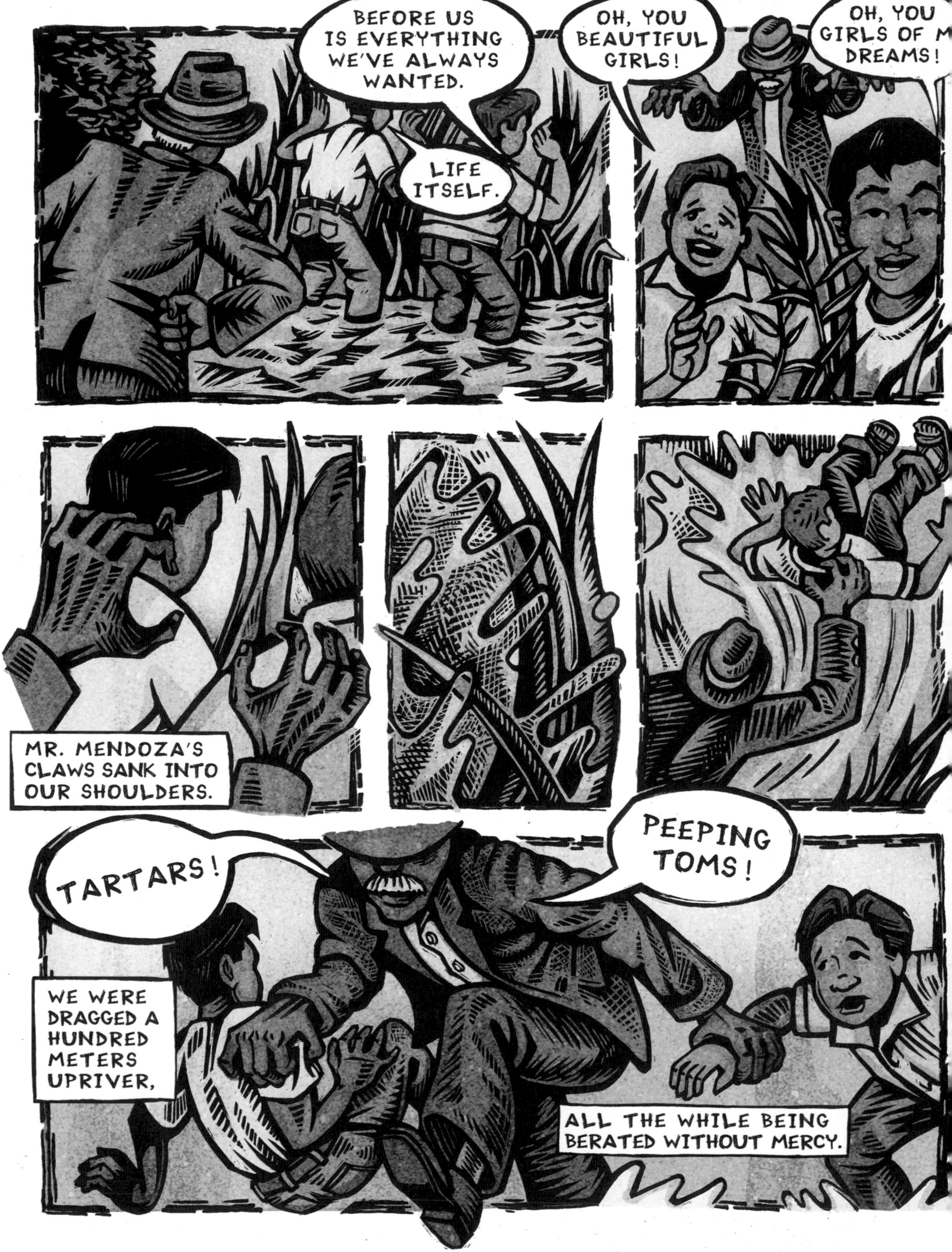
BEFORE US IS EVERYTHING WE'VE ALWAYS WANTED.
LIFE ITSELF.
OH, YOU BEAUTIFUL GIRLS!
OH, YOU GIRLS OF M DREAMS!
MR. MENDOZA'S CLAWS SANK INTO OUR SHOULDERS.
TARTARS!
PEEPING TOMS!
WE WERE DRAGGED A HUNDRED METERS UPRIVER,
ALL THE WHILE BEING BERATED WITHOUT MERCY.

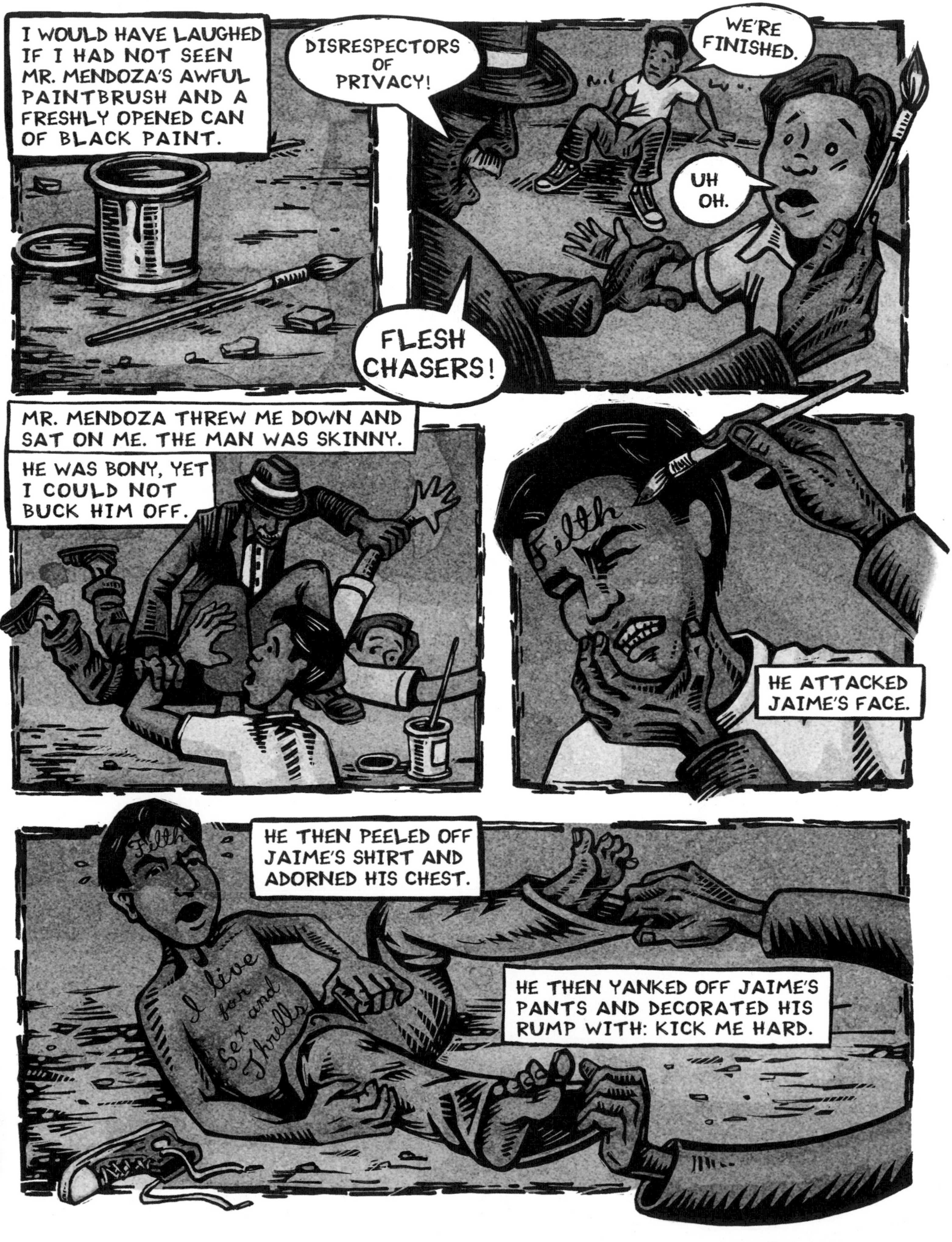
I WOULD HAVE LAUGHED IF I HAD NOT SEEN MR. MENDOZA'S AWFUL PAINTBRUSH AND A FRESHLY OPENED CAN OF BLACK PAINT.
DISRESPECTORS OF PRIVACY!
WE'RE FINISHED.
UH OH.
FLESH CHASERS!
MR. MENDOZA THREW ME DOWN AND SAT ON ME. THE MAN WAS SKINNY.
HE WAS BONY, YET I COULD NOT BUCK HIM OFF.
Filth
HE ATTACKED JAIME'S FACE.
HE THEN PEELED OFF JAIME'S SHIRT AND ADORNED HIS CHEST.
Filth
I live for Sex and Thrills
HE THEN YANKED OFF JAIME'S PANTS AND DECORATED HIS RUMP WITH: KICK ME HARD.

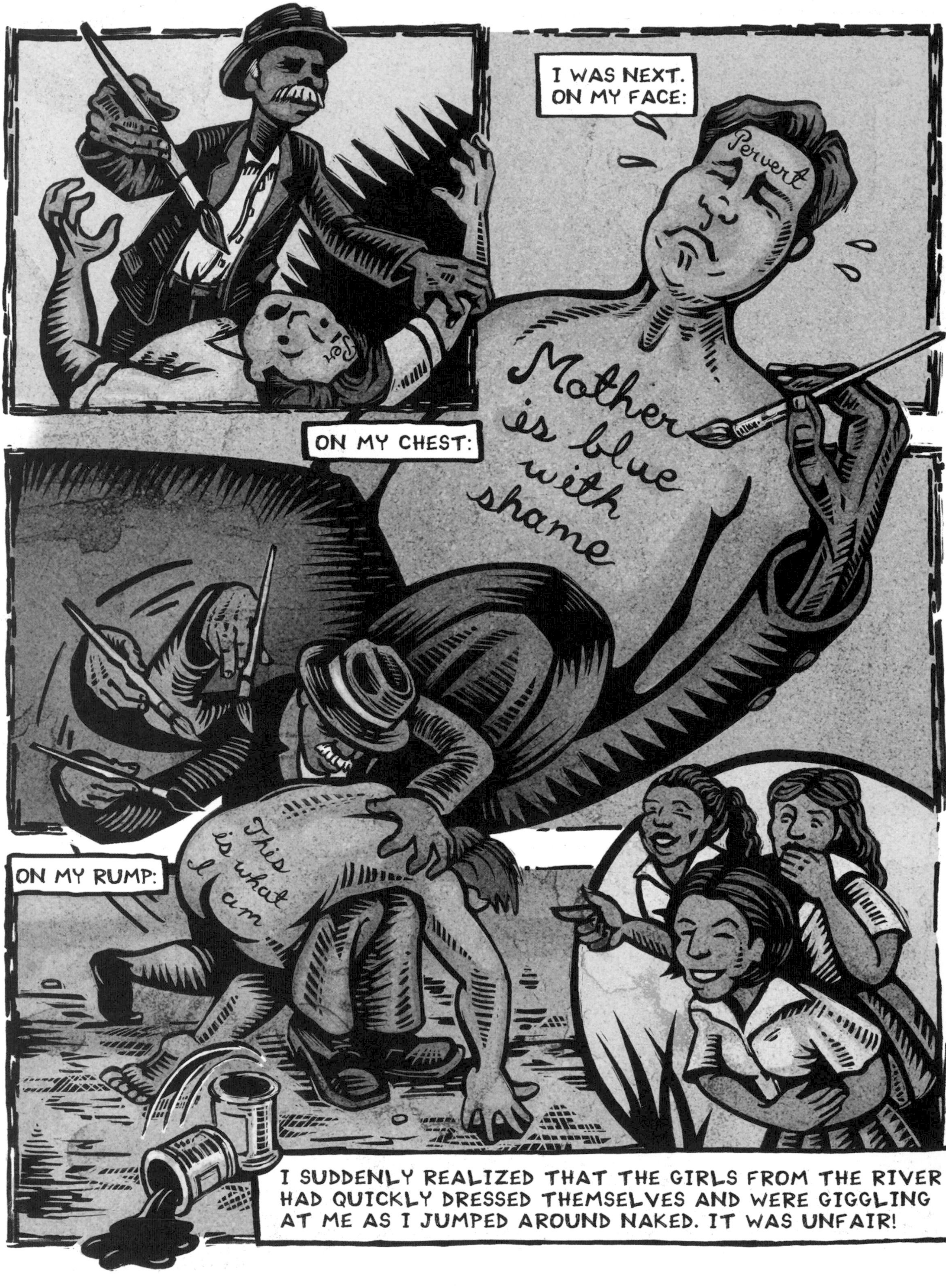
I WAS NEXT. ON MY FACE:
Pervert
ON MY CHEST:
Mother is blue with shame
ON MY RUMP:
This is what I am
I SUDDENLY REALIZED THAT THE GIRLS FROM THE RIVER HAD QUICKLY DRESSED THEMSELVES AND WERE GIGGLING AT ME AS I JUMPED AROUND NAKED. IT WAS UNFAIR!

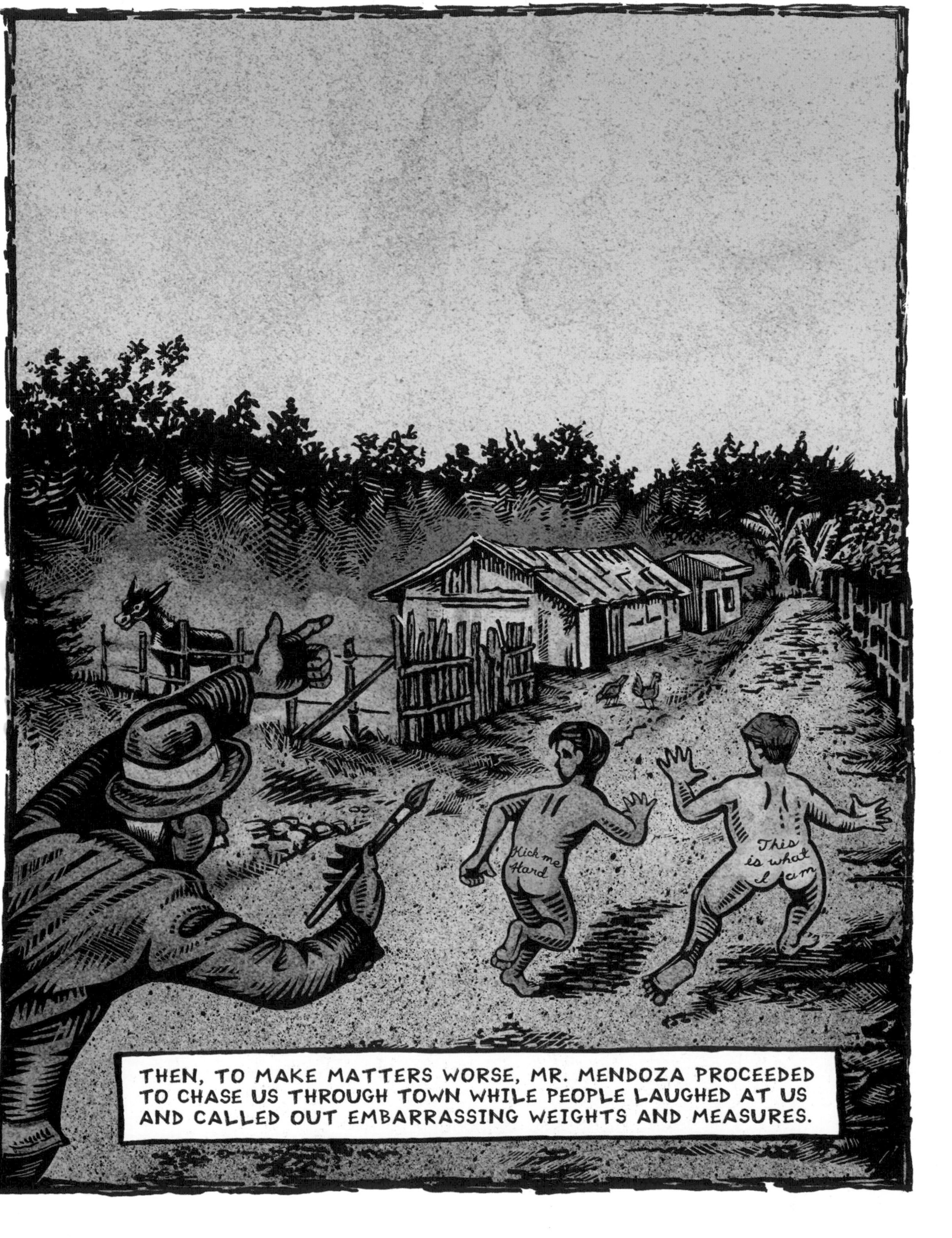
Kick me Hard
This is what I am
THEN, TO MAKE MATTERS WORSE, MR. MENDOZA PROCEEDED TO CHASE US THROUGH TOWN WHILE PEOPLE LAUGHED AT US AND CALLED OUT EMBARRASSING WEIGHTS AND MEASURES.

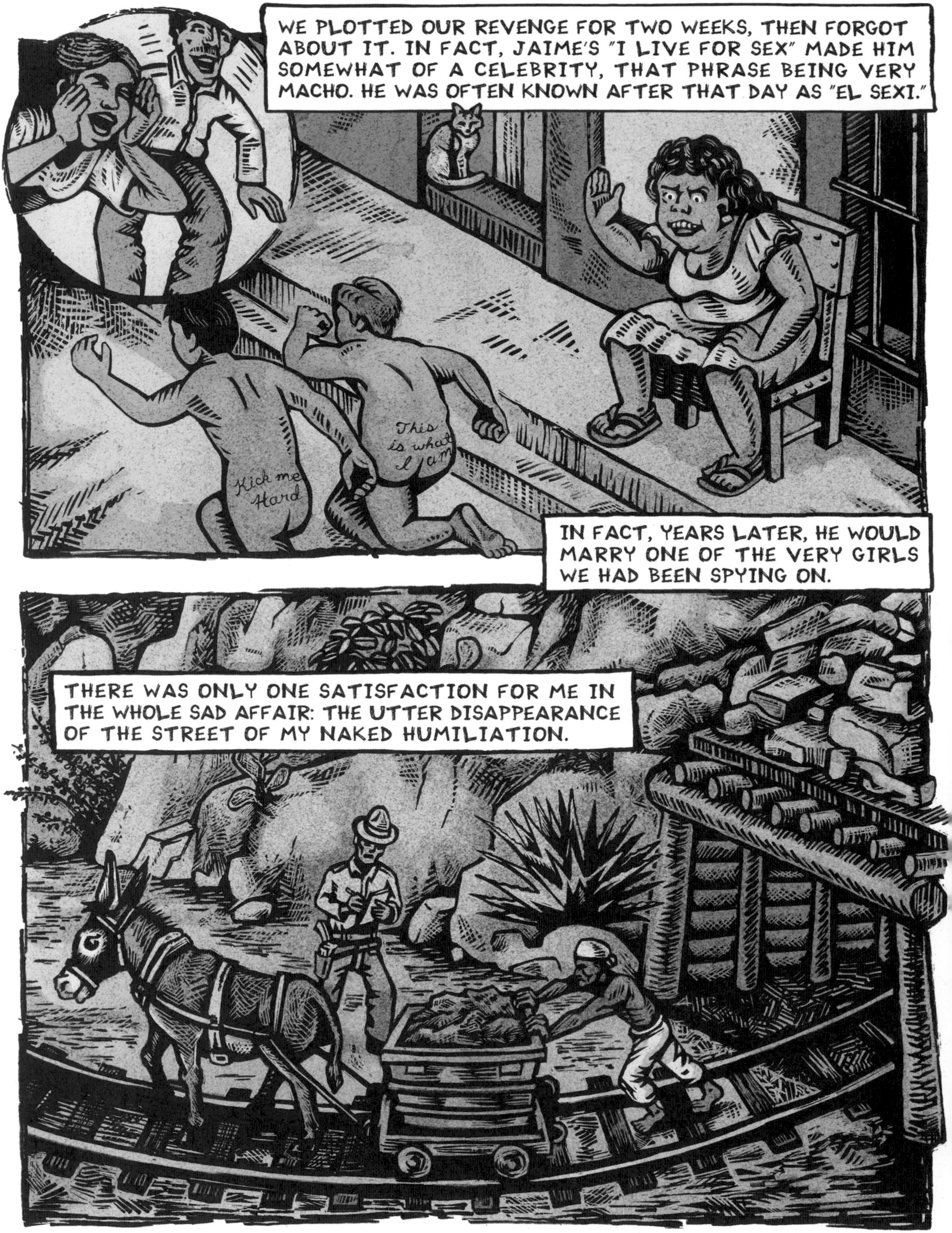
WE PLOTTED OUR REVENGE FOR TWO WEEKS, THEN FORGOT ABOUT IT. IN FACT, JAIME'S "I LIVE FOR SEX" MADE HIM SOMEWHAT OF A CELEBRITY, THAT PHRASE BEING VERY MACHO. HE WAS OFTEN KNOWN AFTER THAT DAY AS "EL SEXI."
Kick me Hard
This is what I am
IN FACT, YEARS LATER, HE WOULD MARRY ONE OF THE VERY GIRLS WE HAD BEEN SPYING ON.
THERE WAS ONLY ONE SATISFACTION FOR ME IN THE WHOLE SAD AFFAIR: THE UTTER DISAPPEARANCE OF THE STREET OF MY NAKED HUMILIATION.

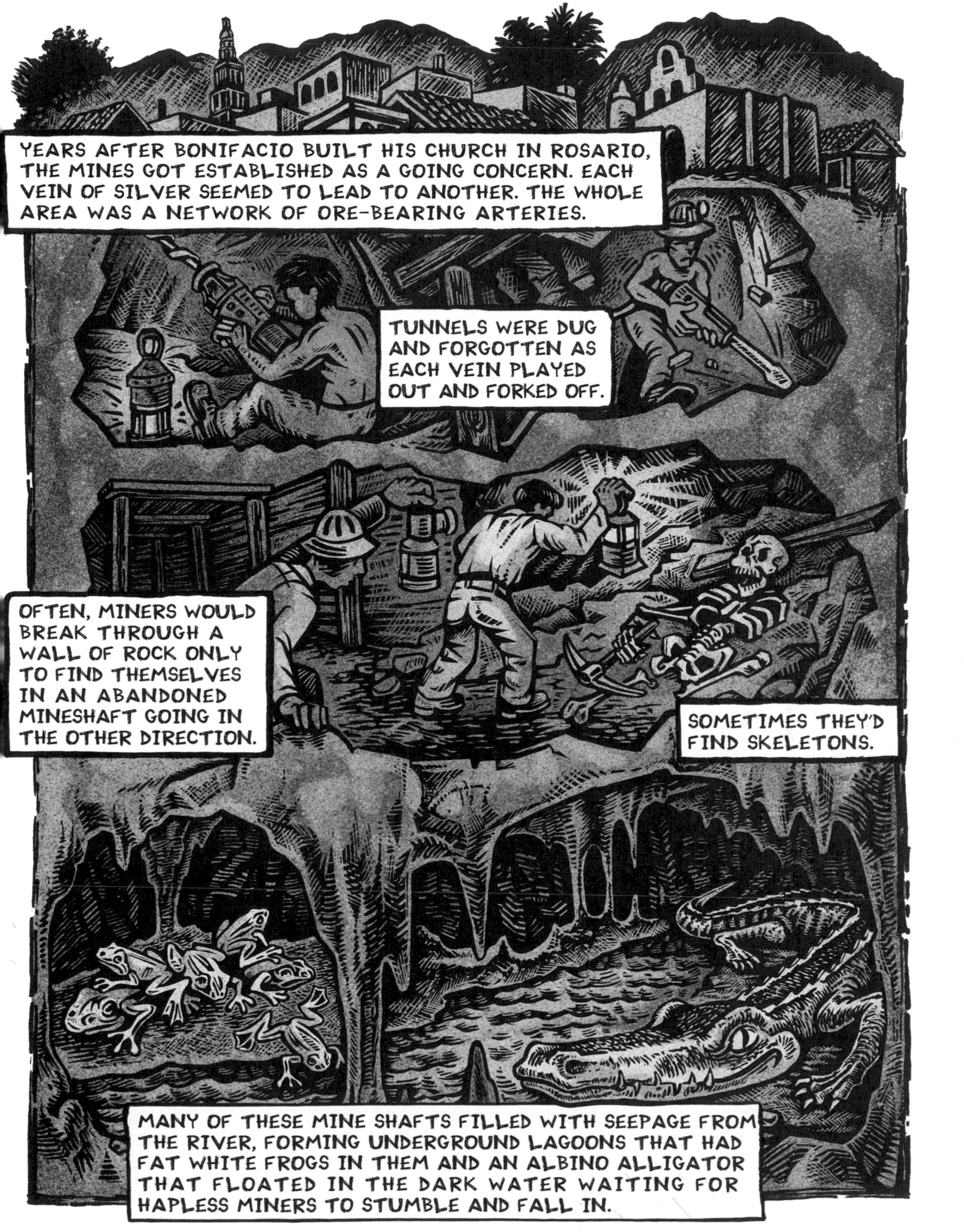
YEARS AFTER BONIFACIO BUILT HIS CHURCH IN ROSARIO, THE MINES GOT ESTABLISHED AS A GOING CONCERN. EACH VEIN OF SILVER SEEMED TO LEAD TO ANOTHER. THE WHOLE AREA WAS A NETWORK OF ORE-BEARING ARTERIES.
TUNNELS WERE DUG AND FORGOTTEN AS EACH VEIN PLAYED OUT AND FORKED OFF.
OFTEN, MINERS WOULD BREAK THROUGH A WALL OF ROCK ONLY TO FIND THEMSELVES IN AN ABANDONED MINESHAFT GOING IN THE OTHER DIRECTION.
SOMETIMES THEY'D FIND SKELETONS.
MANY OF THESE MINE SHAFTS FILLED WITH SEEPAGE FROM THE RIVER, FORMING UNDERGROUND LAGOONS THAT HAD FAT WHITE FROGS IN THEM AND AN ALBINO ALLIGATOR THAT FLOATED IN THE DARK WATER WAITING FOR HAPLESS MINERS TO STUMBLE AND FALL IN.

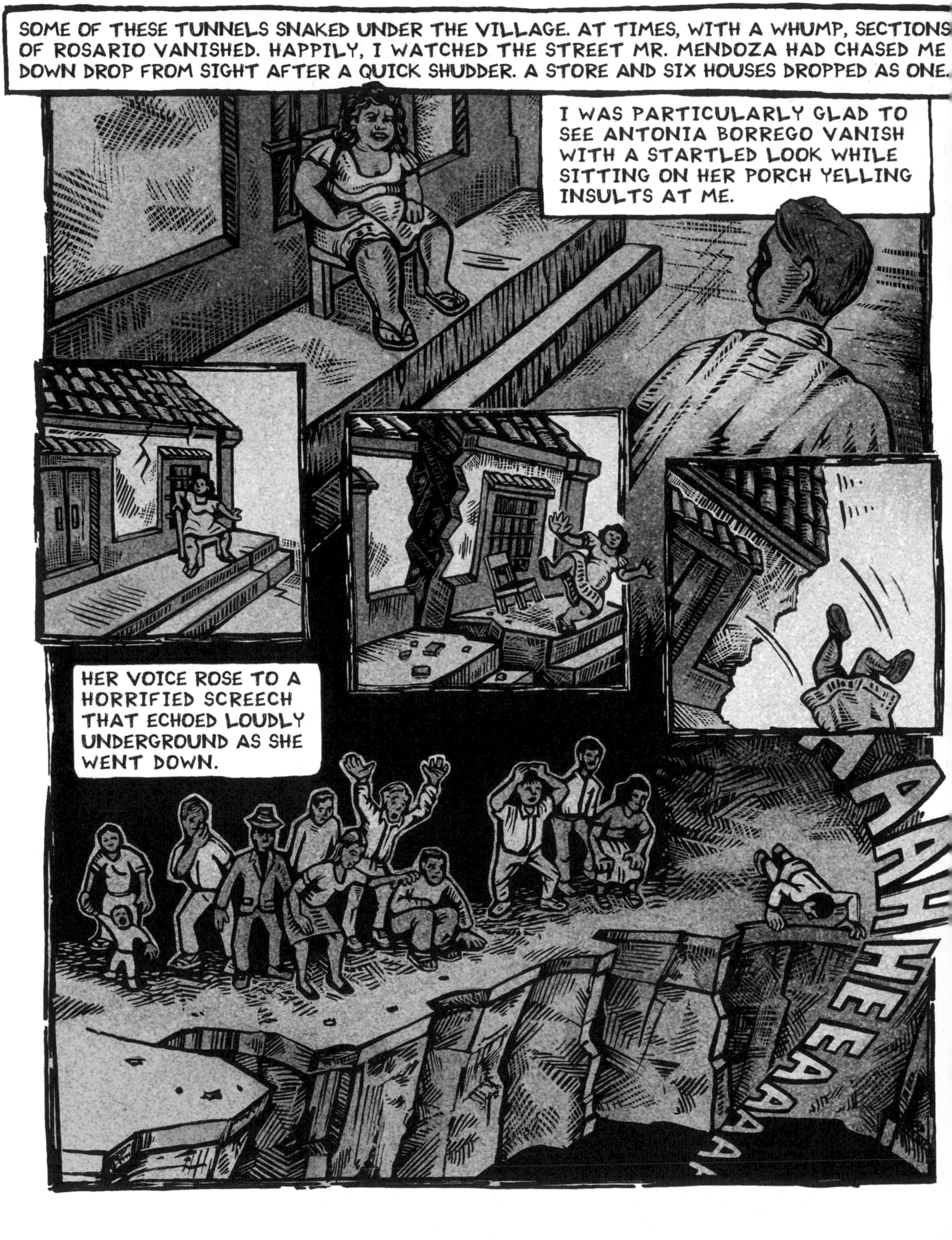
SOME OF THESE TUNNELS SNAKED UNDER THE VILLAGE. AT TIMES, WITH A WHUMP, SECTIONS OF ROSARIO VANISHED. HAPPILY, I WATCHED THE STREET MR. MENDOZA HAD CHASED ME DOWN DROP FROM SIGHT AFTER A QUICK SHUDDER. A STORE AND SIX HOUSES DROPPED AS ONE.
I WAS PARTICULARLY GLAD TO SEE ANTONIA BORREGO VANISH WITH A STARTLED LOOK WHILE SITTING ON HER PORCH YELLING INSULTS AT ME.
HER VOICE ROSE TO A HORRIFIED SCREECH THAT ECHOED LOUDLY UNDERGROUND AS SHE WENT DOWN.
AAAHHEEAAAAA

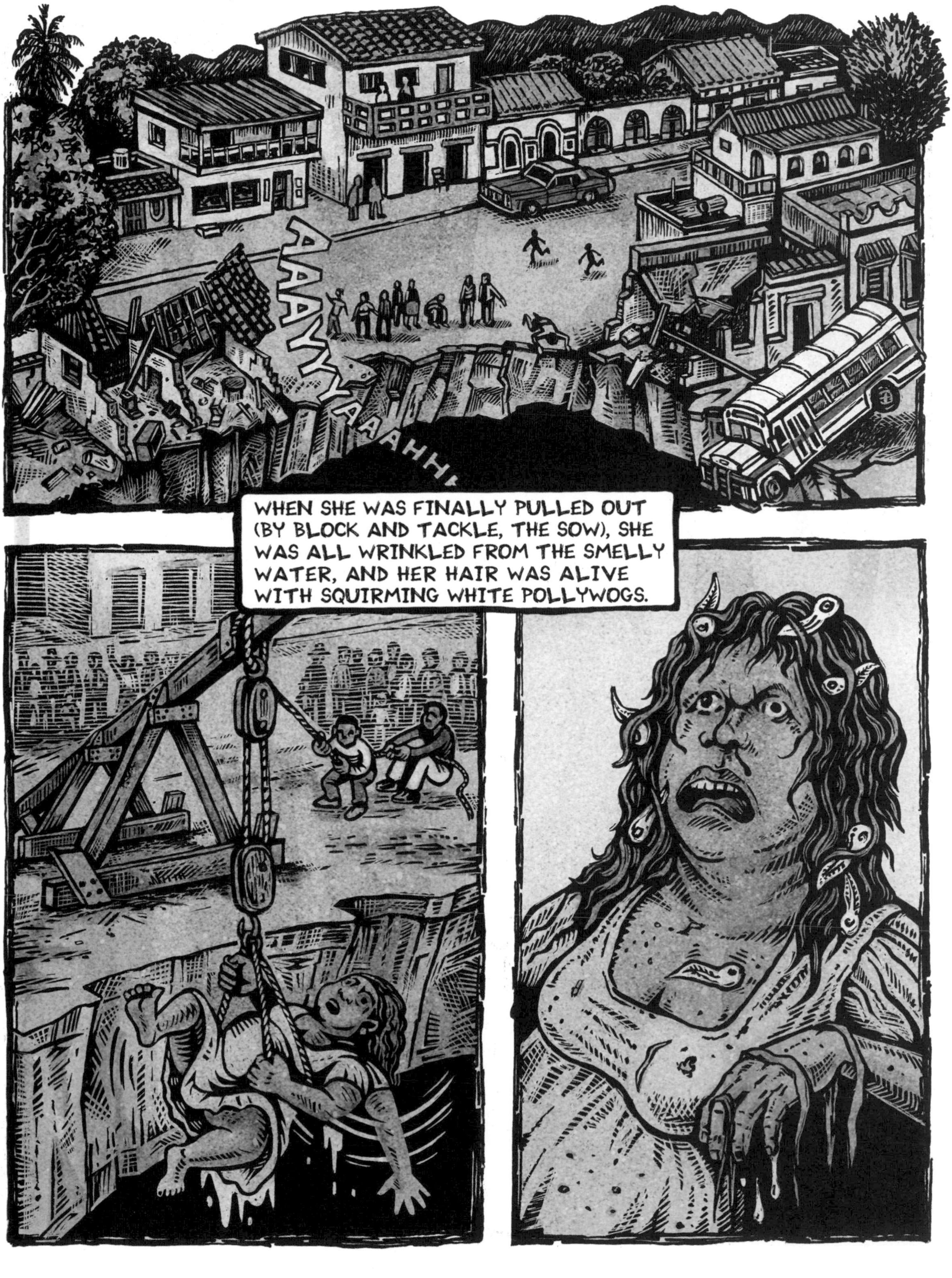
AAAYYYAAAHH
WHEN SHE WAS FINALLY PULLED OUT (BY BLOCK AND TACKLE, THE SOW), SHE WAS ALL WRINKLED FROM THE SMELLY WATER, AND HER HAIR WAS ALIVE WITH SQUIRMING WHITE POLLYWOGS.

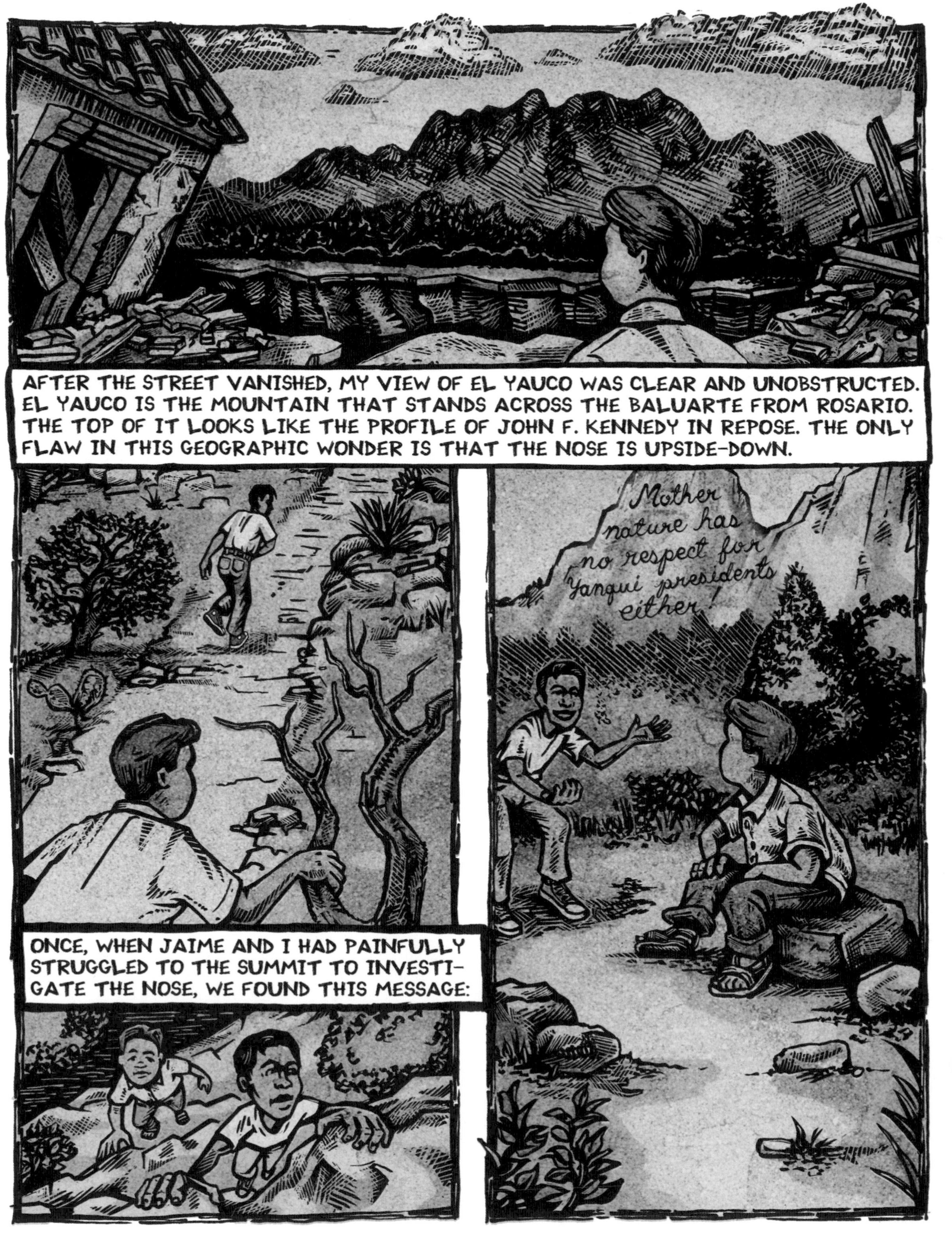
AFTER THE STREET VANISHED, MY VIEW OF EL YAUCO WAS CLEAR AND UNOBSTRUCTED. EL YAUCO IS THE MOUNTAIN THAT STANDS ACROSS THE BALUARTE FROM ROSARIO. THE TOP OF IT LOOKS LIKE THE PROFILE OF JOHN F. KENNEDY IN REPOSE. THE ONLY FLAW IN THIS GEOGRAPHIC WONDER IS THAT THE NOSE IS UPSIDE-DOWN.
ONCE, WHEN JAIME AND I HAD PAINFULLY STRUGGLED TO THE SUMMIT TO INVESTIGATE THE NOSE, WE FOUND THIS MESSAGE:
Mother nature has no respect for Yanqui presidents either!

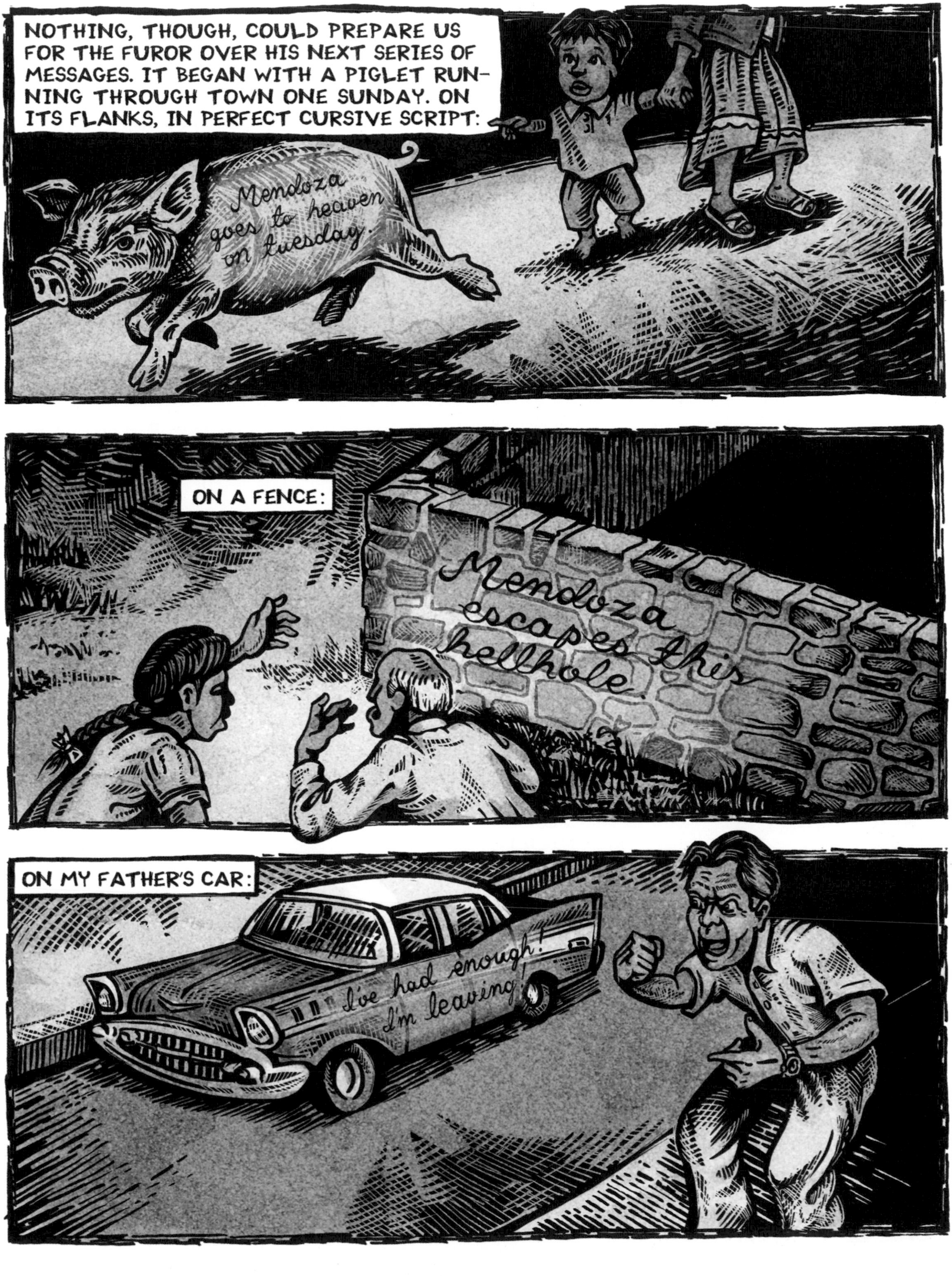
NOTHING, THOUGH, COULD PREPARE US FOR THE FUROR OVER HIS NEXT SERIES OF MESSAGES. IT BEGAN WITH A PIGLET RUNNING THROUGH TOWN ONE SUNDAY. ON ITS FLANKS, IN PERFECT CURSIVE SCRIPT:
Mendoza goes to heaven on tuesday.
ON A FENCE:
Mendoza escapes this hellhole
ON MY FATHER'S CAR:
I've had enough! I'm leaving!

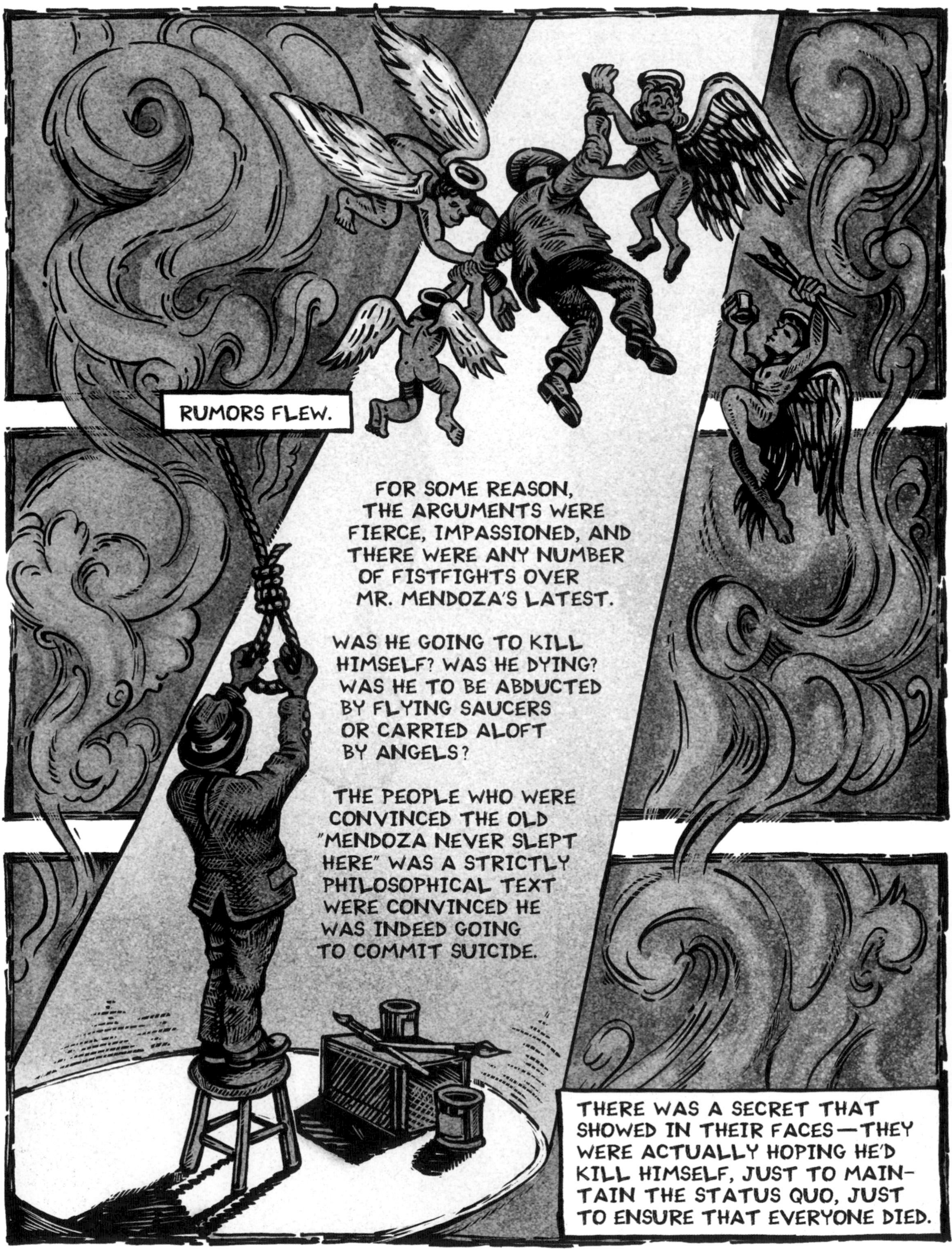
RUMORS FLEW.
FOR SOME REASON, THE ARGUMENTS WERE FIERCE, IMPASSIONED, AND THERE WERE ANY NUMBER OF FISTFIGHTS OVER MR. MENDOZA'S LATEST.
WAS HE GOING TO KILL HIMSELF? WAS HE DYING? WAS HE TO BE ABDUCTED BY FLYING SAUCERS OR CARRIED ALOFT BY ANGELS?
THE PEOPLE WHO WERE CONVINCED THE OLD "MENDOZA NEVER SLEPT HERE" WAS A STRICTLY PHILOSOPHICAL TEXT WERE CONVINCED HE WAS INDEED GOING TO COMMIT SUICIDE.
THERE WAS A SECRET THAT SHOWED IN THEIR FACES—THEY WERE ACTUALLY HOPING HE'D KILL HIMSELF, JUST TO MAINTAIN THE STATUS QUO, JUST TO ENSURE THAT EVERYONE DIED.

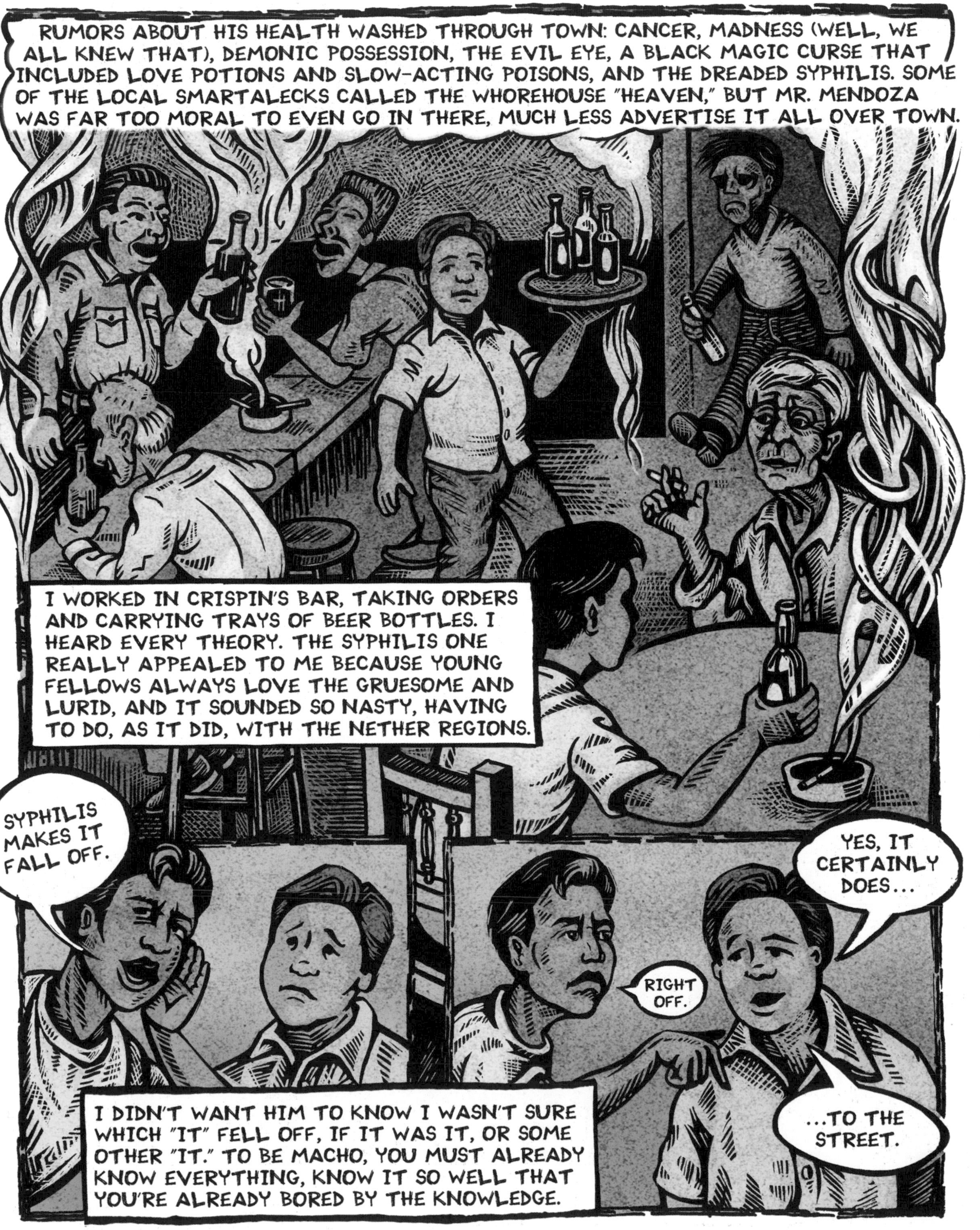
RUMORS ABOUT HIS HEALTH WASHED THROUGH TOWN: CANCER, MADNESS (WELL, WE ALL KNEW THAT), DEMONIC POSSESSION, THE EVIL EYE, A BLACK MAGIC CURSE THAT INCLUDED LOVE POTIONS AND SLOW-ACTING POISONS, AND THE DREADED SYPHILIS. SOME OF THE LOCAL SMARTALECKS CALLED THE WHOREHOUSE "HEAVEN," BUT MR. MENDOZA WAS FAR TOO MORAL TO EVEN GO IN THERE, MUCH LESS ADVERTISE IT ALL OVER TOWN.
I WORKED IN CRISPIN'S BAR, TAKING ORDERS AND CARRYING TRAYS OF BEER BOTTLES. I HEARD EVERY THEORY. THE SYPHILIS ONE REALLY APPEALED TO ME BECAUSE YOUNG FELLOWS ALWAYS LOVE THE GRUESOME AND LURID, AND IT SOUNDED SO NASTY, HAVING TO DO, AS IT DID, WITH THE NETHER REGIONS.
SYPHILIS MAKES IT FALL OFF.
RIGHT OFF.
YES, IT CERTAINLY DOES...
...TO THE STREET.
I DIDN'T WANT HIM TO KNOW I WASN'T SURE WHICH "IT" FELL OFF, IF IT WAS IT, OR SOME OTHER "IT." TO BE MACHO, YOU MUST ALREADY KNOW EVERYTHING, KNOW IT SO WELL THAT YOU'RE ALREADY BORED BY THE KNOWLEDGE.

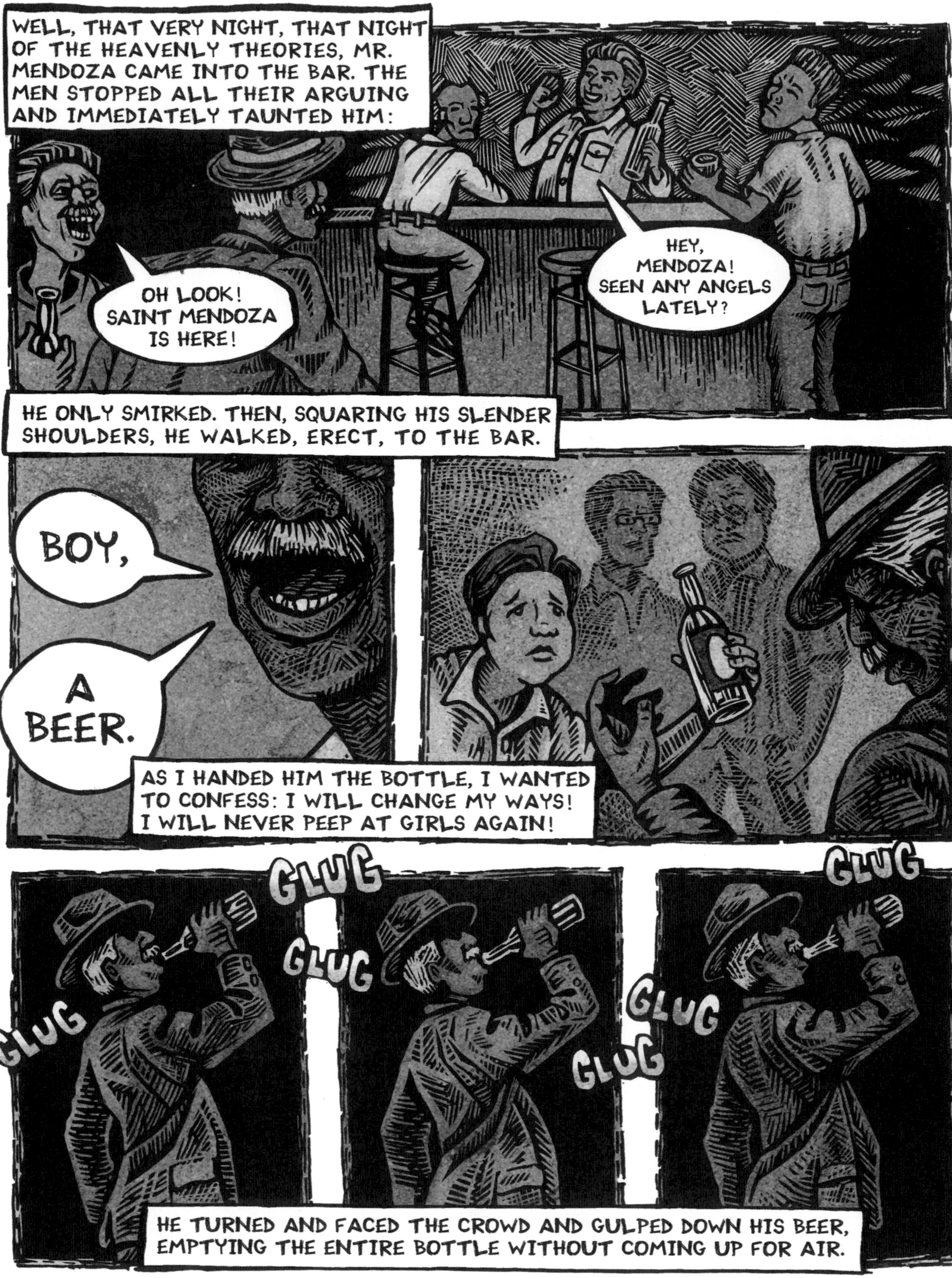
WELL, THAT VERY NIGHT, THAT NIGHT OF THE HEAVENLY THEORIES, MR. MENDOZA CAME INTO THE BAR. THE MEN STOPPED ALL THEIR ARGUING AND IMMEDIATELY TAUNTED HIM:
OH LOOK! SAINT MENDOZA IS HERE!
HEY, MENDOZA! SEEN ANY ANGELS LATELY?
HE ONLY SMIRKED. THEN, SQUARING HIS SLENDER SHOULDERS, HE WALKED, ERECT, TO THE BAR.
BOY,
A BEER.
AS I HANDED HIM THE BOTTLE, I WANTED TO CONFESS: I WILL CHANGE MY WAYS! I WILL NEVER PEEP AT GIRLS AGAIN!
GLUG
GLUG
GLUG
GLUG
GLUG
GLUG
HE TURNED AND FACED THE CROWD AND GULPED DOWN HIS BEER, EMPTYING THE ENTIRE BOTTLE WITHOUT COMING UP FOR AIR.

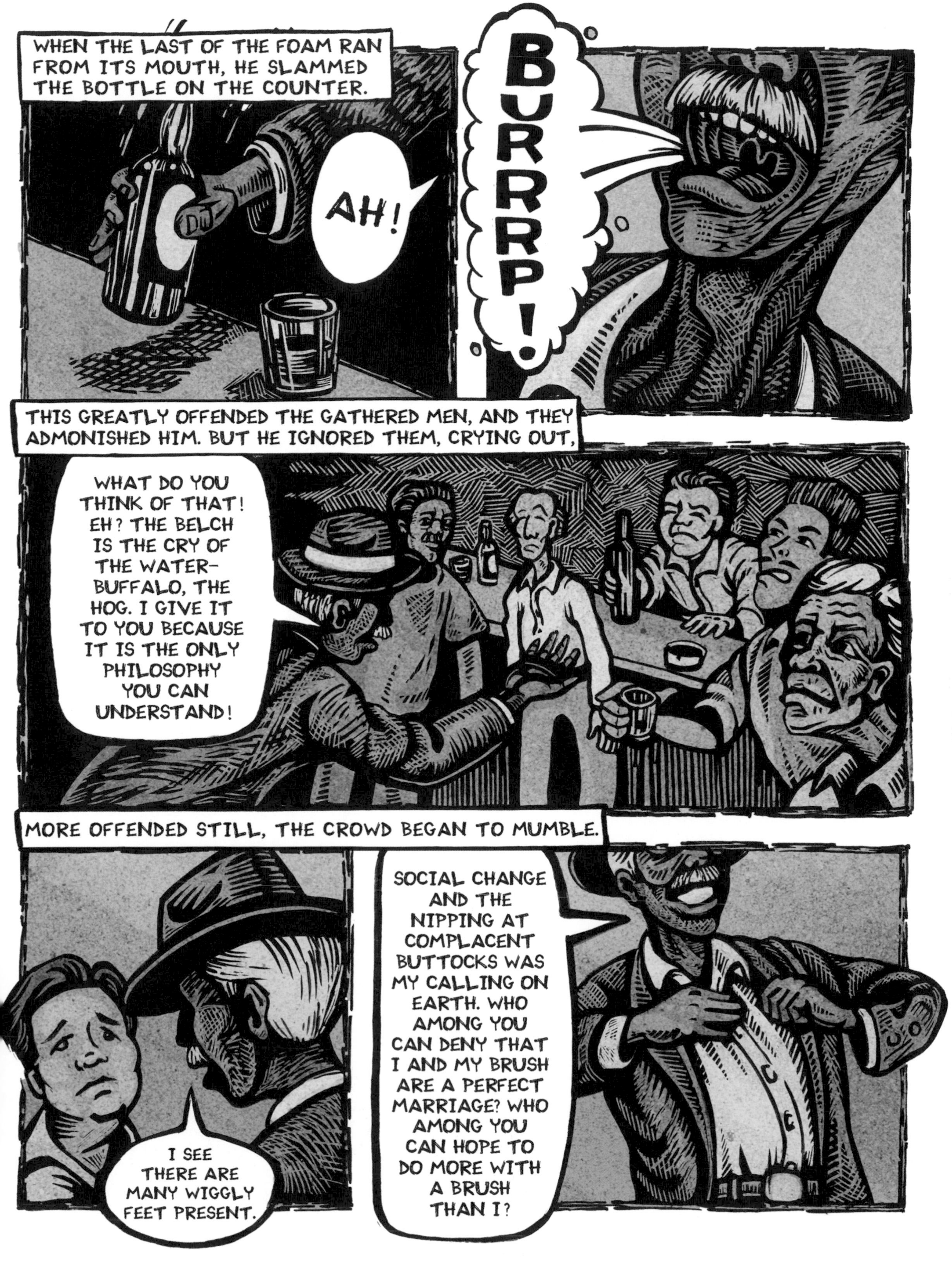

WHEN THE LAST OF THE FOAM RAN FROM ITS MOUTH, HE SLAMMED THE BOTTLE ON THE COUNTER.
AH!
BURRRP!
THIS GREATLY OFFENDED THE GATHERED MEN, AND THEY ADMONISHED HIM. BUT HE IGNORED THEM, CRYING OUT,
WHAT DO YOU THINK OF THAT! EH? THE BELCH IS THE CRY OF THE WATER-BUFFALO, THE HOG. I GIVE IT TO YOU BECAUSE IT IS THE ONLY PHILOSOPHY YOU CAN UNDERSTAND!
MORE OFFENDED STILL, THE CROWD BEGAN TO MUMBLE.
I SEE THERE ARE MANY WIGGLY FEET PRESENT.
SOCIAL CHANGE AND THE NIPPING AT COMPLACENT BUTTOCKS WAS MY CALLING ON EARTH. WHO AMONG YOU CAN DENY THAT I AND MY BRUSH ARE A PERFECT MARRIAGE? WHO AMONG YOU CAN HOPE TO DO MORE WITH A BRUSH THAN I?

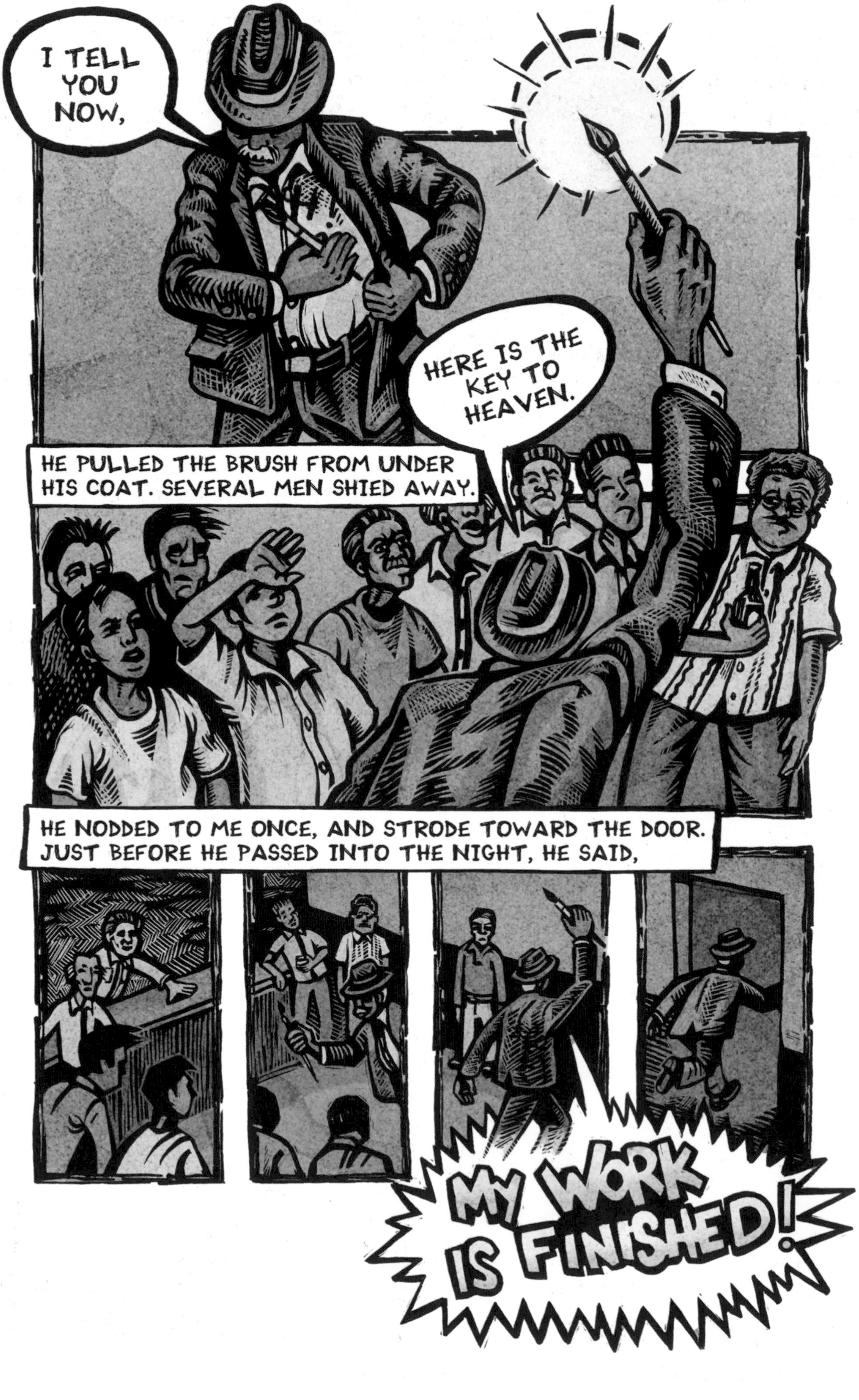
I TELL YOU NOW,
HERE IS THE KEY TO HEAVEN.
HE PULLED THE BRUSH FROM UNDER HIS COAT. SEVERAL MEN SHIED AWAY.
HE NODDED TO ME ONCE, AND STRODE TOWARD THE DOOR. JUST BEFORE HE PASSED INTO THE NIGHT, HE SAID,
MY WORK IS FINISHED!

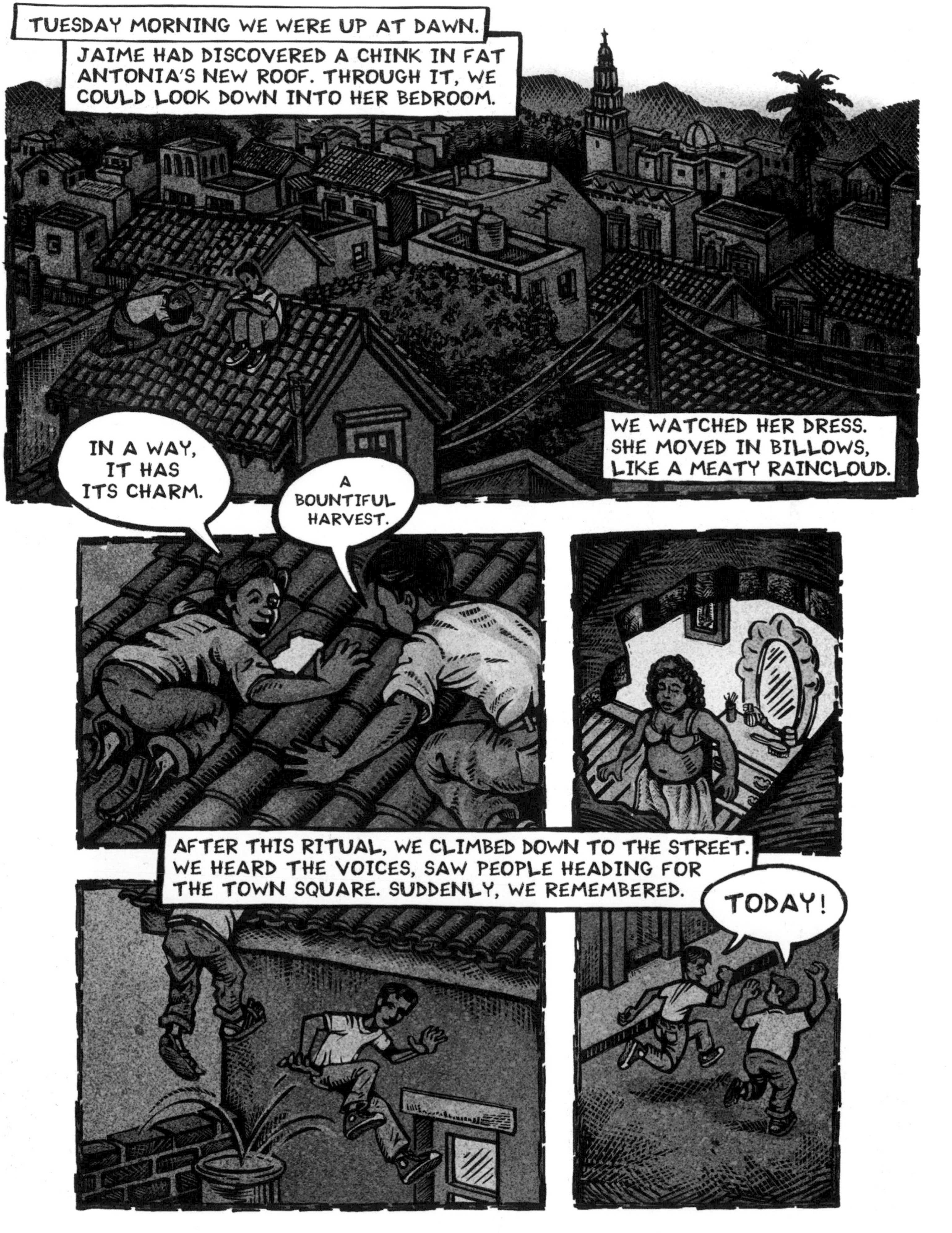
TUESDAY MORNING WE WERE UP AT DAWN.
JAIME HAD DISCOVERED A CHINK IN FAT ANTONIA'S NEW ROOF. THROUGH IT, WE COULD LOOK DOWN INTO HER BEDROOM.
WE WATCHED HER DRESS. SHE MOVED IN BILLOWS, LIKE A MEATY RAINCLOUD.
IN A WAY, IT HAS ITS CHARM.
A BOUNTIFUL HARVEST.
AFTER THIS RITUAL, WE CLIMBED DOWN TO THE STREET. WE HEARD THE VOICES, SAW PEOPLE HEADING FOR THE TOWN SQUARE. SUDDENLY, WE REMEMBERED.
TODAY!

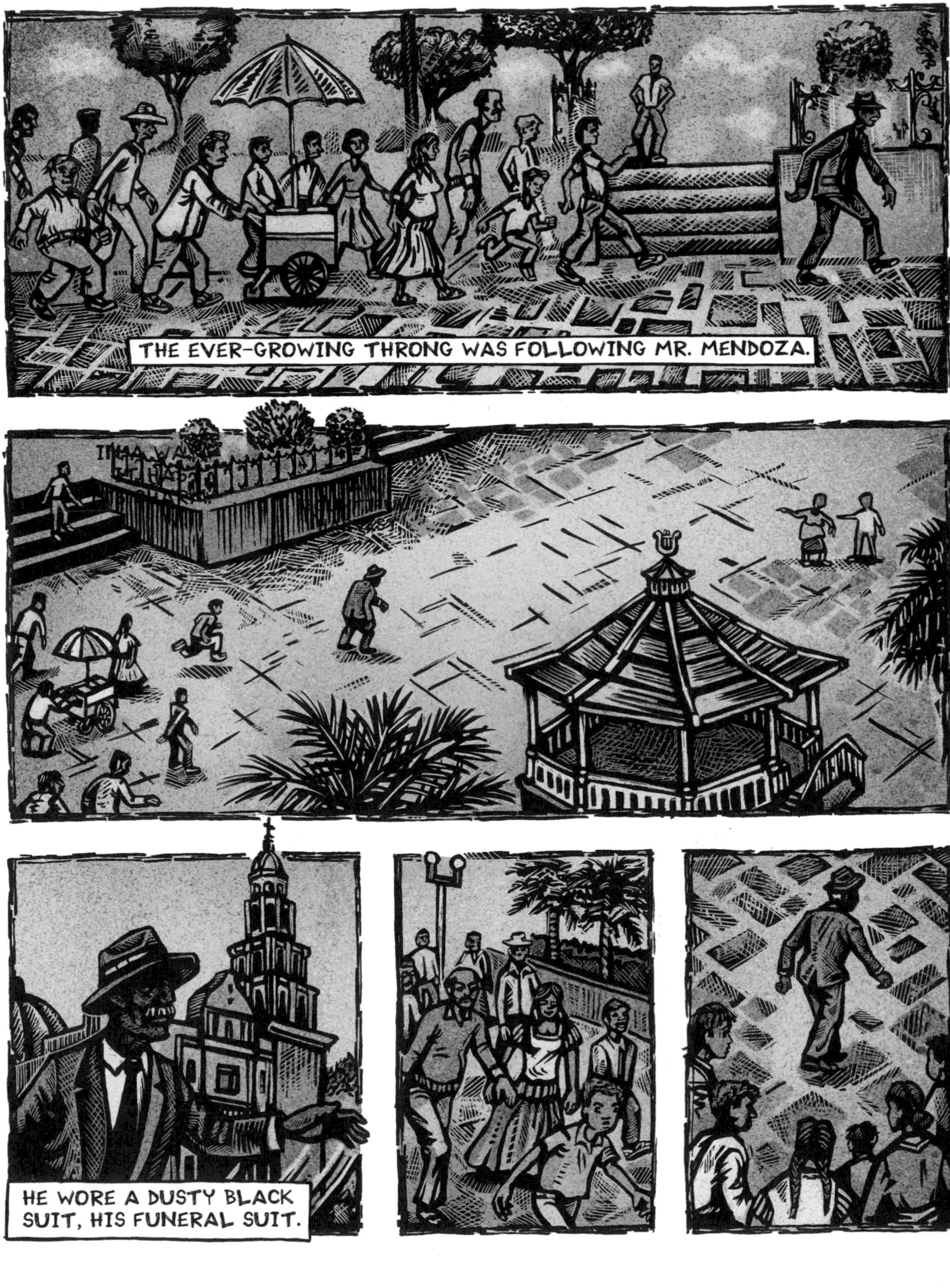
THE EVER-GROWING THRONG WAS FOLLOWING MR. MENDOZA.
HE WORE A DUSTY BLACK SUIT, HIS FUNERAL SUIT.

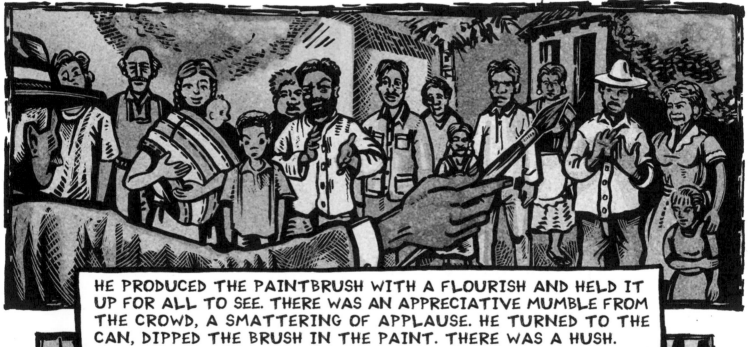

HE PRODUCED THE PAINTBRUSH WITH A FLOURISH AND HELD IT UP FOR ALL TO SEE. THERE WAS AN APPRECIATIVE MUMBLE FROM THE CROWD, A SMATTERING OF APPLAUSE. HE TURNED TO THE CAN, DIPPED THE BRUSH IN THE PAINT. THERE WAS A HUSH.

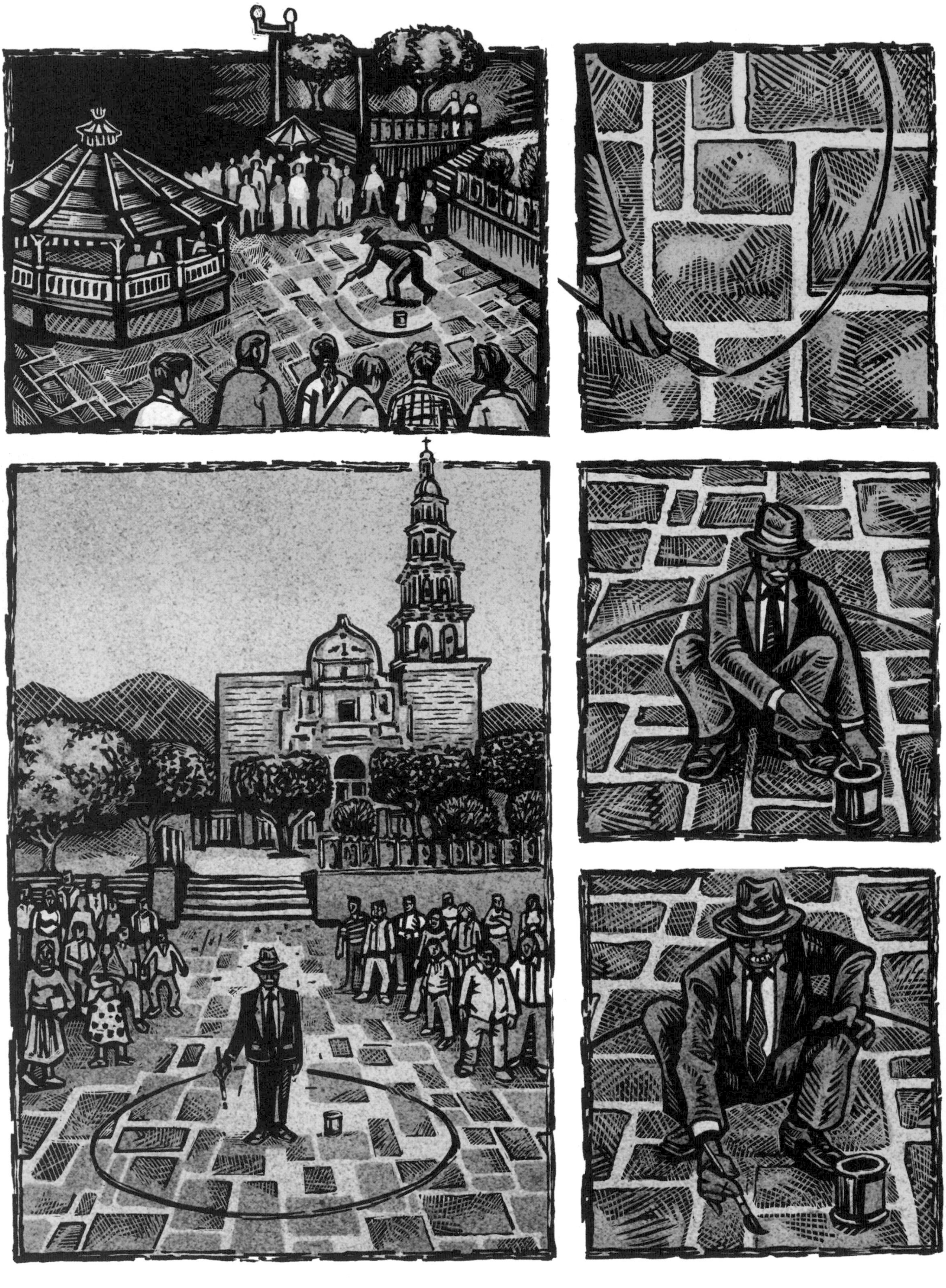

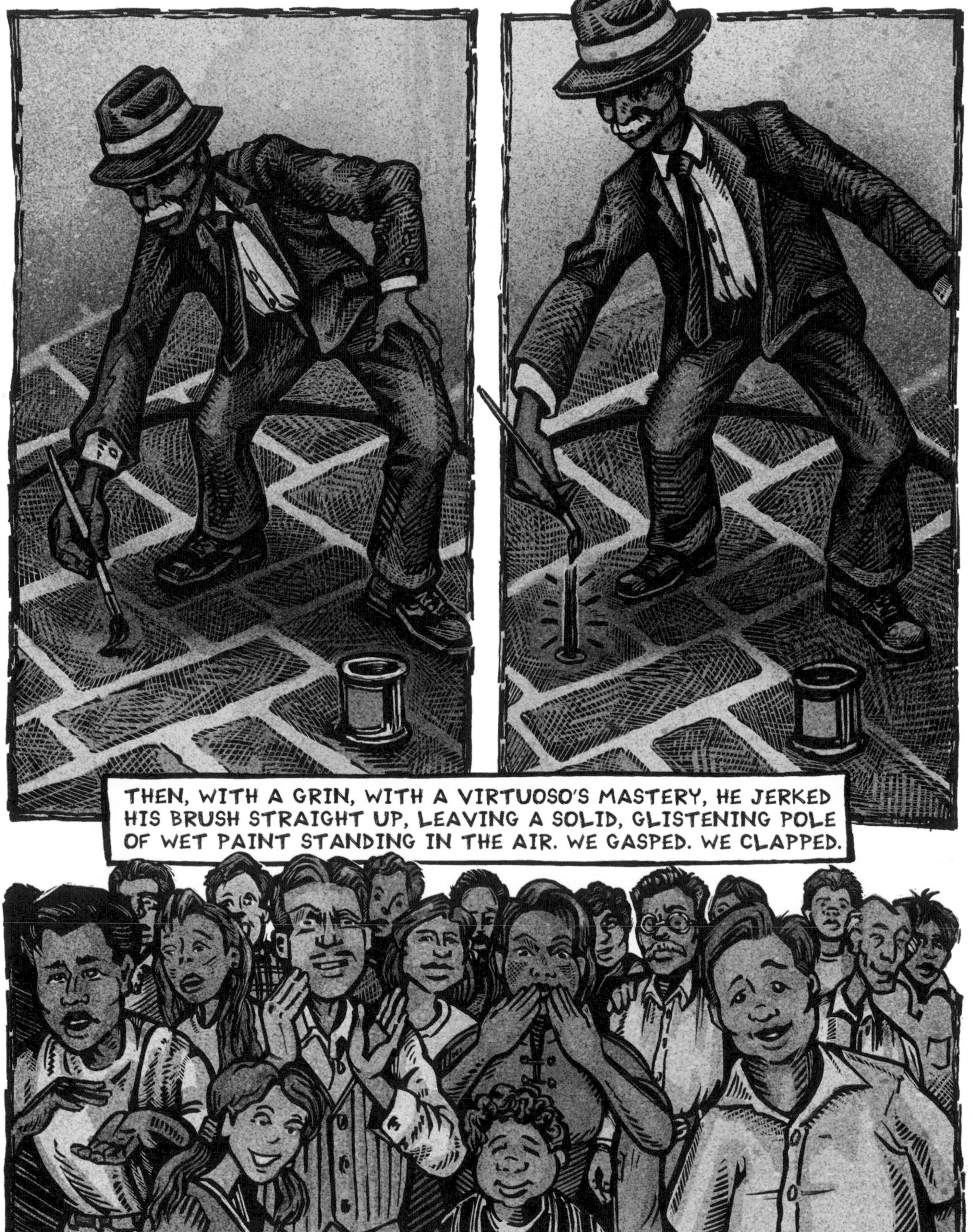
THEN, WITH A GRIN, WITH A VIRTUOSO'S MASTERY, HE JERKED HIS BRUSH STRAIGHT UP, LEAVING A SOLID, GLISTENING POLE OF WET PAINT STANDING IN THE AIR. WE GASPED. WE CLAPPED.

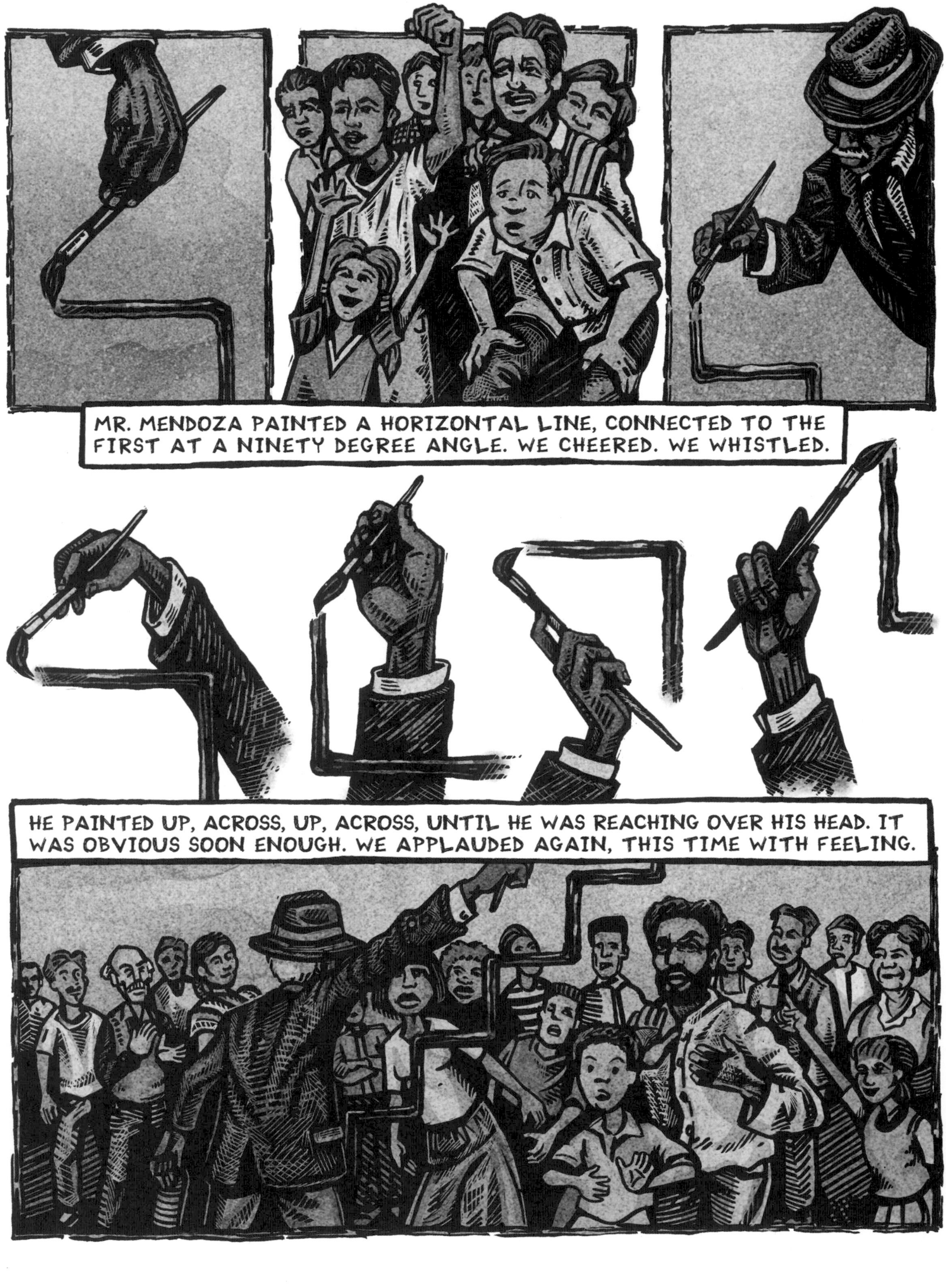
MR. MENDOZA PAINTED A HORIZONTAL LINE, CONNECTED TO THE FIRST AT A NINETY DEGREE ANGLE. WE CHEERED. WE WHISTLED.
HE PAINTED UP, ACROSS, UP, ACROSS, UNTIL HE WAS REACHING OVER HIS HEAD. IT WAS OBVIOUS SOON ENOUGH. WE APPLAUDED AGAIN, THIS TIME WITH FEELING.

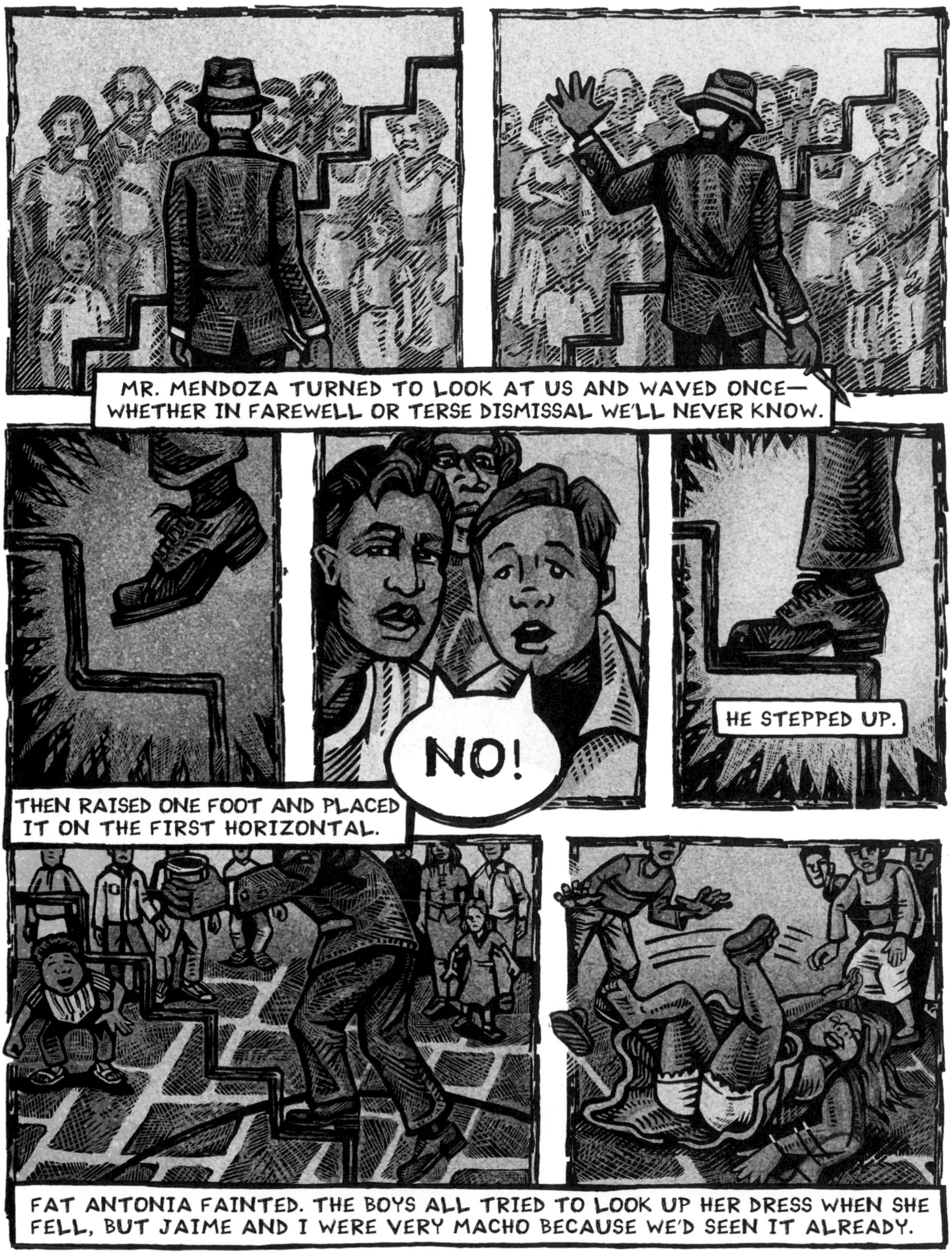
MR. MENDOZA TURNED TO LOOK AT US AND WAVED ONCE—WHETHER IN FAREWELL OR TERSE DISMISSAL WE'LL NEVER KNOW.
THEN RAISED ONE FOOT AND PLACED IT ON THE FIRST HORIZONTAL.
NO!
HE STEPPED UP.
FAT ANTONIA FAINTED. THE BOYS ALL TRIED TO LOOK UP HER DRESS WHEN SHE FELL, BUT JAIME AND I WERE VERY MACHO BECAUSE WE'D SEEN IT ALREADY.

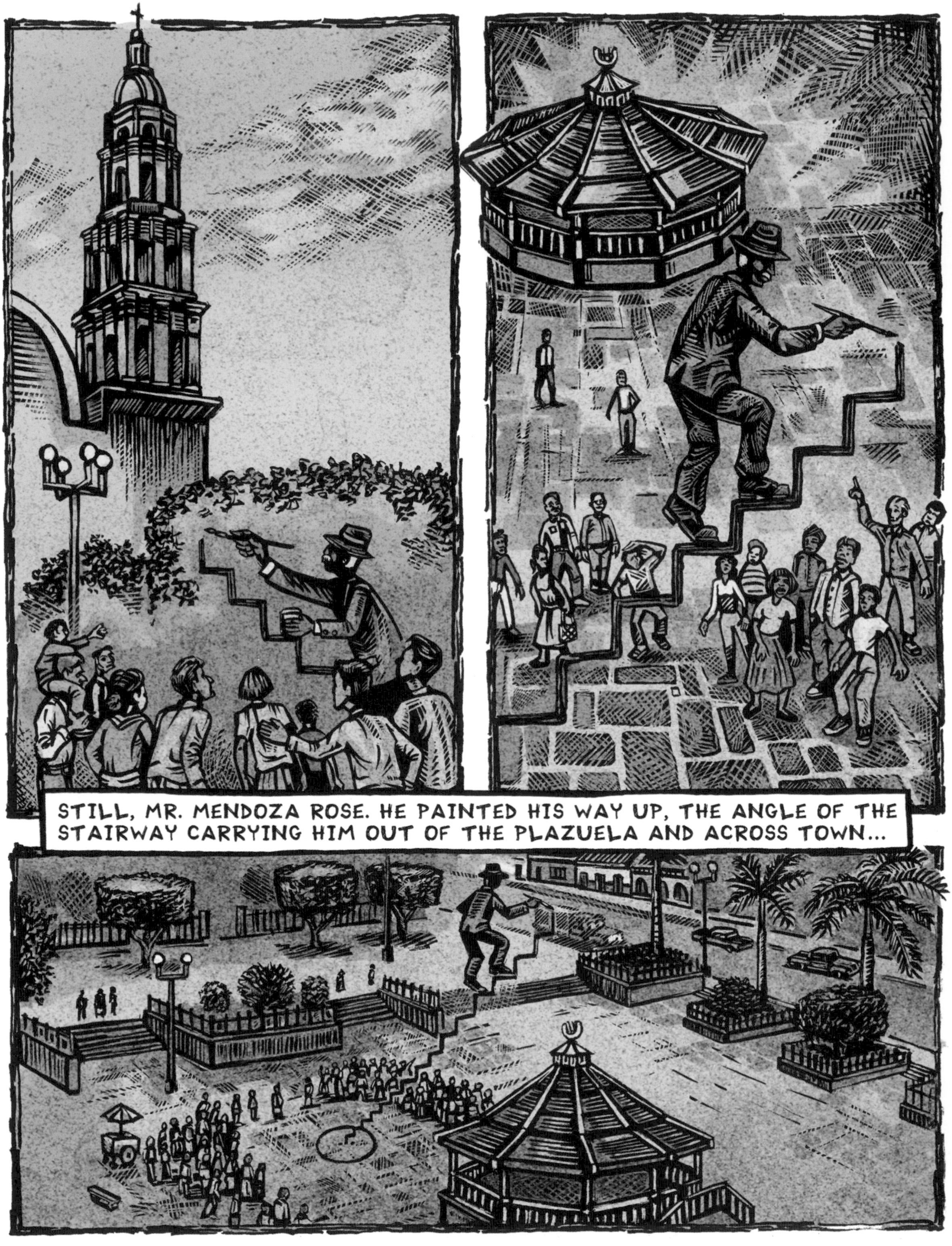
STILL, MR. MENDOZA ROSE. HE PAINTED HIS WAY UP, THE ANGLE OF THE STAIRWAY CARRYING HIM OUT OF THE PLAZUELA AND ACROSS TOWN...

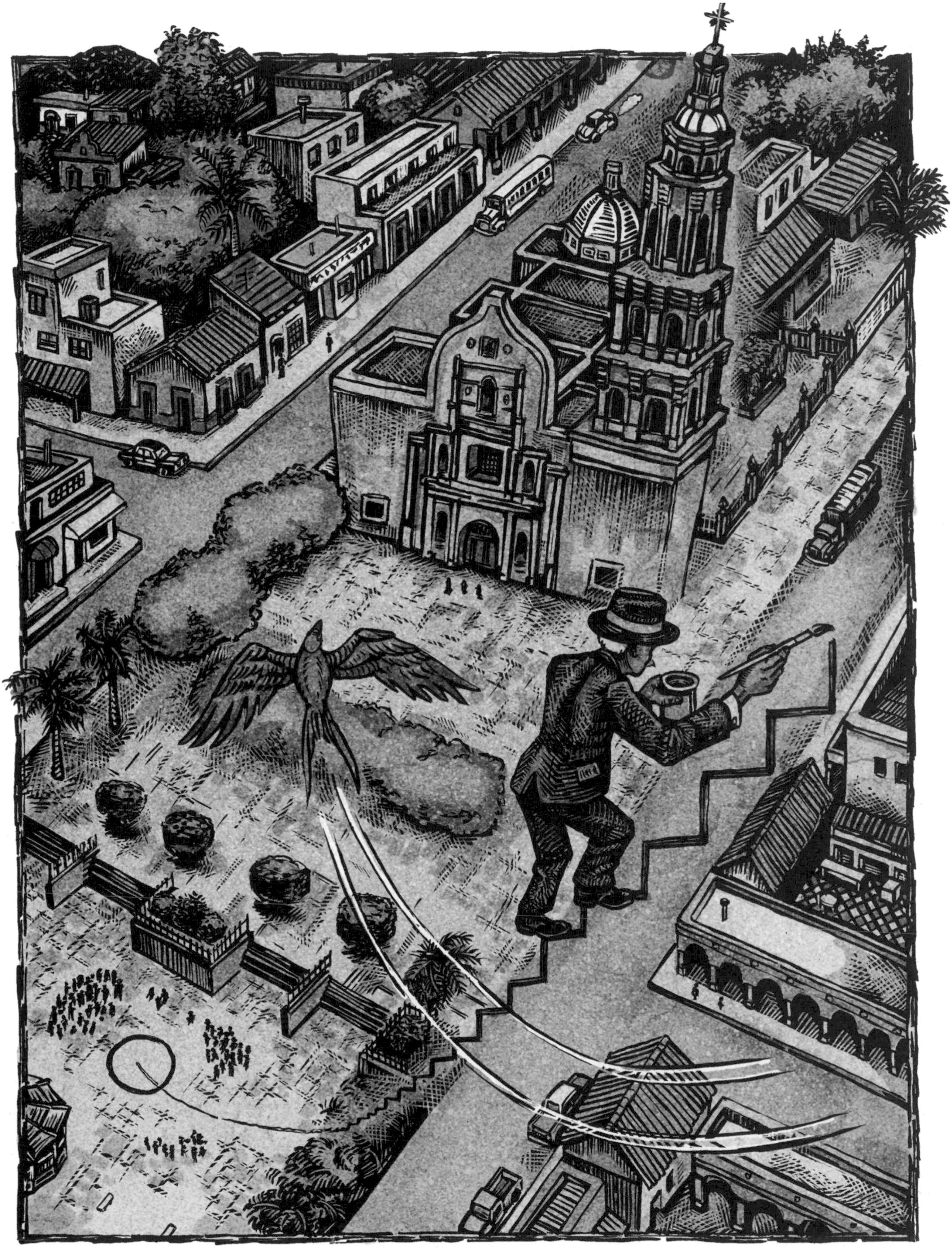

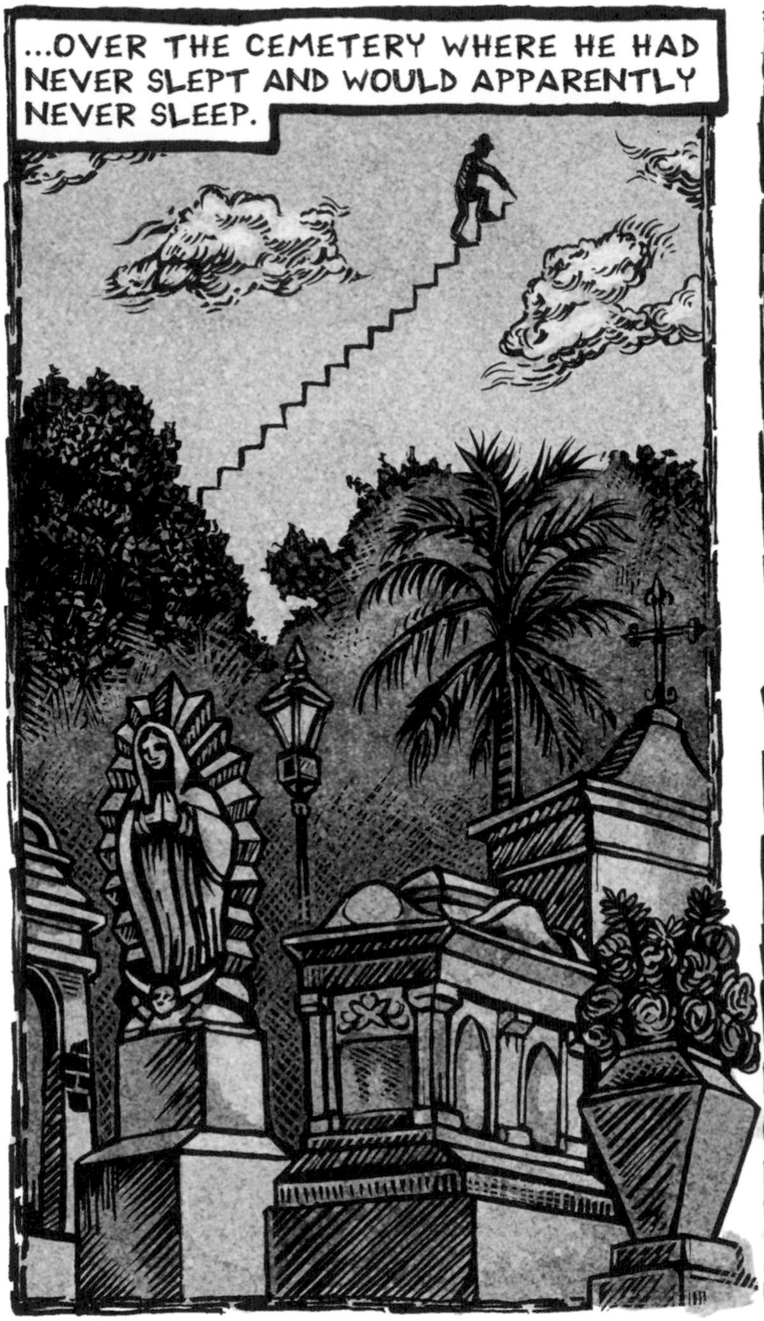
...OVER THE CEMETERY WHERE HE HAD NEVER SLEPT AND WOULD APPARENTLY NEVER SLEEP.

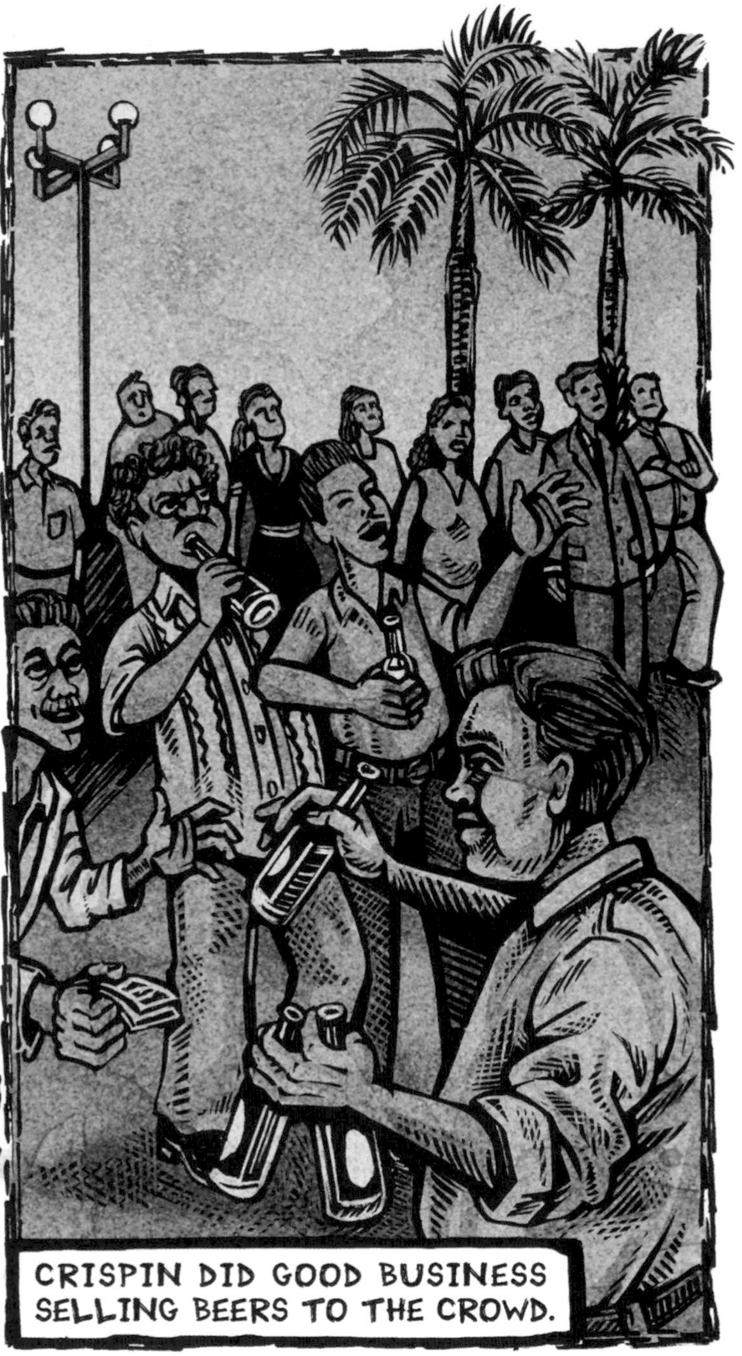
CRISPIN DID GOOD BUSINESS SELLING BEERS TO THE CROWD.

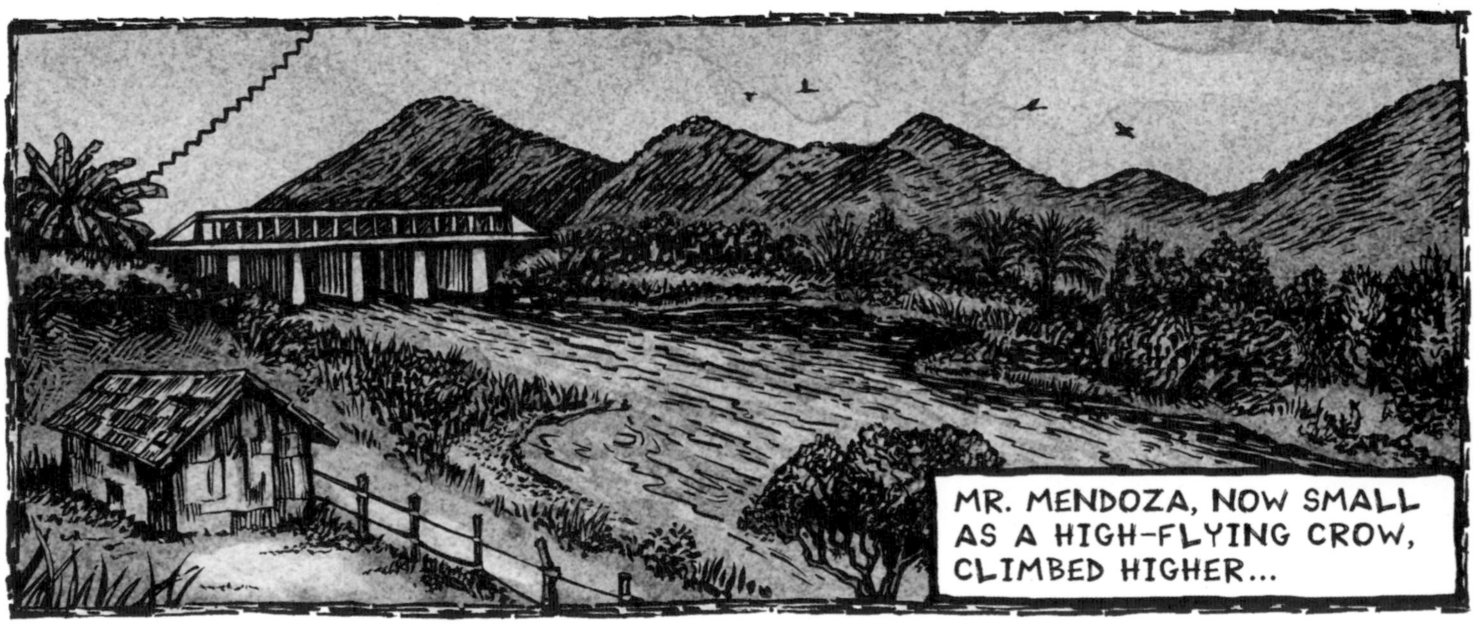
MR. MENDOZA, NOW SMALL AS A HIGH-FLYING CROW, CLIMBED HIGHER...

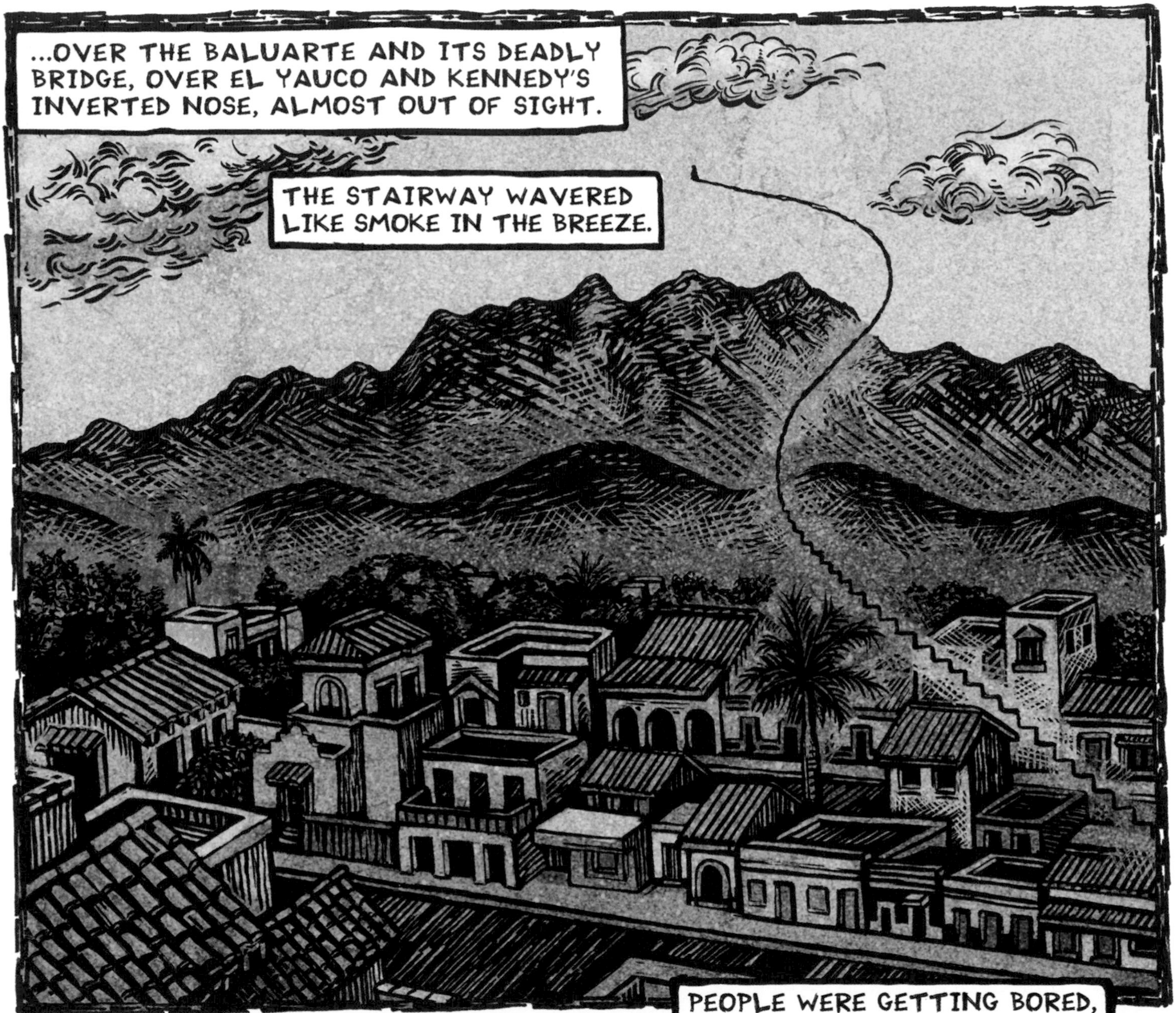
...OVER THE BALUARTE AND ITS DEADLY BRIDGE, OVER EL YAUCO AND KENNEDY'S INVERTED NOSE, ALMOST OUT OF SIGHT.
THE STAIRWAY WAVERED LIKE SMOKE IN THE BREEZE.

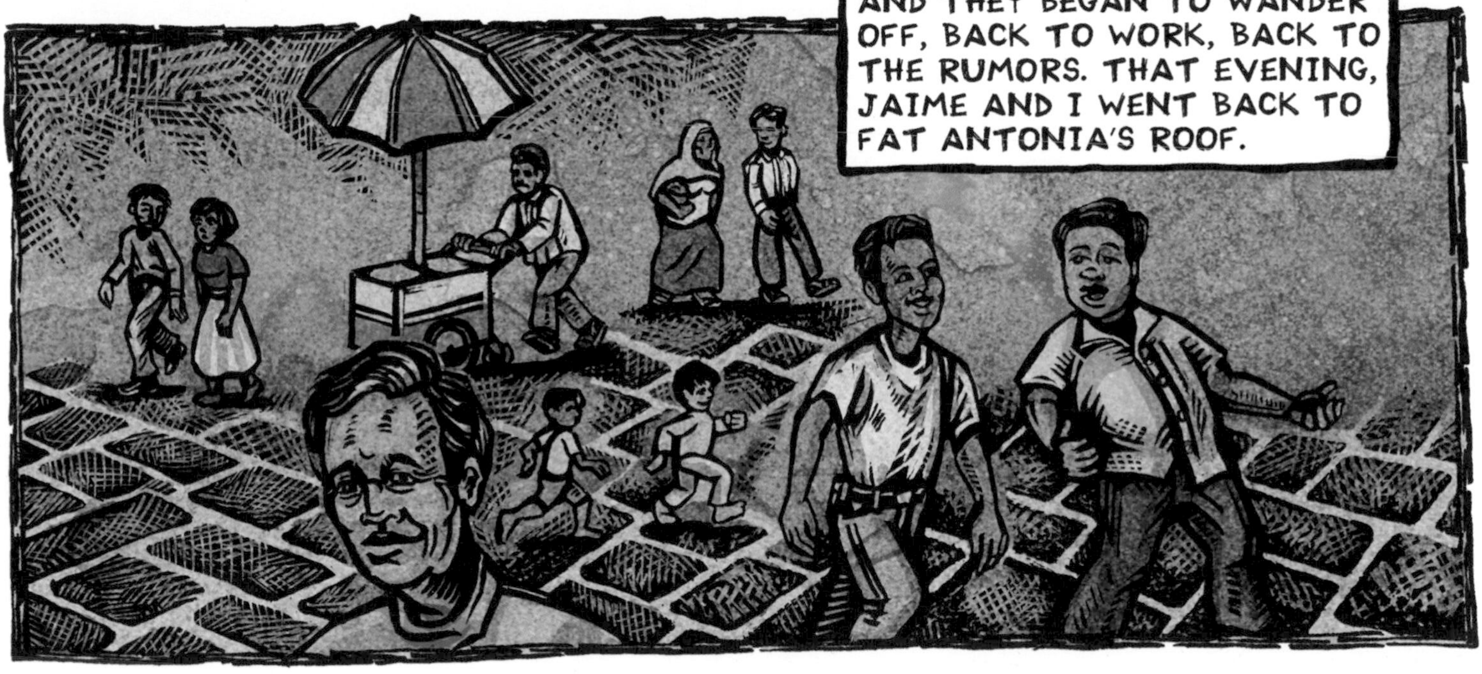
PEOPLE WERE GETTING BORED, AND THEY BEGAN TO WANDER OFF, BACK TO WORK, BACK TO THE RUMORS. THAT EVENING, JAIME AND I WENT BACK TO FAT ANTONIA'S ROOF.

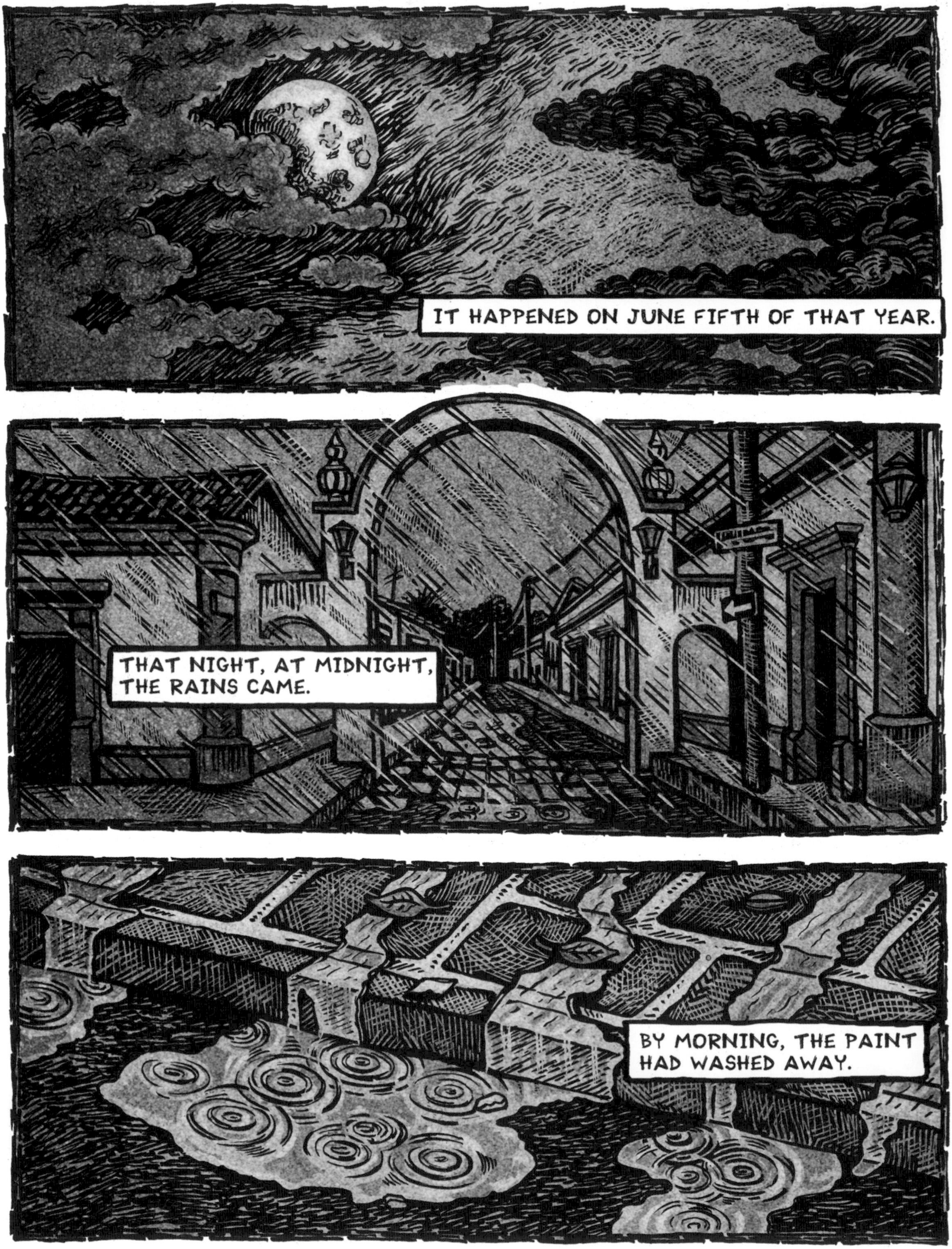
IT HAPPENED ON JUNE FIFTH OF THAT YEAR.
THAT NIGHT, AT MIDNIGHT, THE RAINS CAME.
BY MORNING, THE PAINT HAD WASHED AWAY.

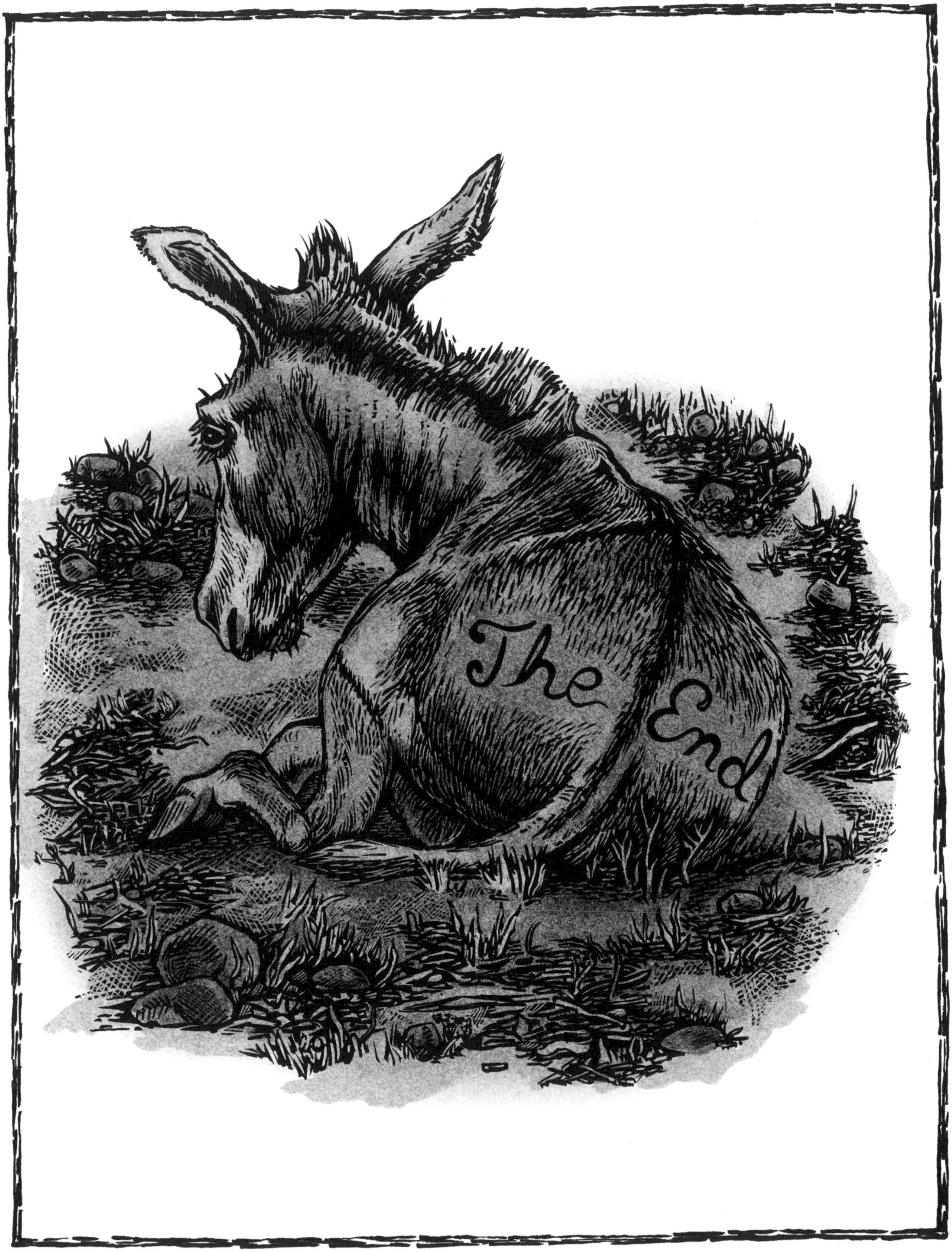
The End

ACKNOWLEDGMENTS

To Anthony Cardinale for his generous assistance and technical expertise in all things computer related; Sharon Kwik and Macéo Cardinale Kwik for being there for me every day and giving me honest feedback; Luis and Cindy Urrea for their enthusiasm and support; Seth Tobocman, Nicole Schulman, Peter Kuper, Sabrina Jones and the rest of the artists from *World War 3 Illustrated* Magazine for helping me grow as a comic book artist; Melissa Jameson, Eric Laursen and Lauren Melodia for supporting me in achieving my goals on a daily basis; Ricardo Galvez and Eland Ward for their friendship and for helping me stay fit; Youme Landowne for being an inspiration and introducing me to the Cinco Puntos family; Colin Moynihan, a good friend; *Punk Planet* Magazine, Groundswell, Blue Mountain Center and Zefrey T.

To my friends in Rosario (Sinaloa, Mexico) who helped with my visual research: Jorge Alberto Hubbard Urrea and his wife, for their generous hospitality and expertise in all things Rosario; Marco Antonio Arriasola and his wife Hayde at Ciber La Plazuela; Guillermina Perez Aguiar for the home-cooked meals, homemade cheese and tour of the abandoned mines; Carmine Galindo Lizaraga and Maria del Rosario Flores Galindo of Hotel Galindo; Saul Carillo and Maria Felix Morales, my traveling vendor friends from Zacatecas; and the beautiful town of Rosario itself.

— C.C.

LUIS ALBERTO URREA is the author of the widely acclaimed novel *The Hummingbird's Daughter* and a 2005 Pulitzer Prize finalist for nonfiction for *The Devil's Highway*. Inducted into the Latino Literature Hall of Fame, Luis was born in Tijuana, Mexico to a Mexican father and an American mother.

CHRISTOPHER CARDINALE is a cartoonist and community muralist with a social justice message. He has painted large-scale murals opposing war and corporate globalization and promoting community values and social-economic justice in New York, Italy, Greece and Mexico. He lives in Brooklyn. His website is christophercardinale.com.